POPULAR MECHANICS

125

WAYS TO HANDLE AND PREVENT HOME HAZARDS AND EMERGENCIES

POPULAR MECHANICS

125

WAYS TO HANDLE AND PREVENT HOME HAZARDS AND EMERGENCIES

GARY BRANSON

Illustrations by Ron Carboni

HEARST BOOKS

New York

Library of Congress Cataloging-in-Publication Data

Branson, Gary D.
    Popular mechanics 125 ways to handle and prevent home hazards and emergencies / Gary Branson ; illustrations by Ron Carboni. Illustrations on pages 174–175 © George Retseck
        p.   cm.
    Includes index.
    ISBN 0–688–12785–1
    1. Home accidents—Prevention.   I. Title.
TX150.B68   1993
643'.028'9—dc20   93–11706
                                                               CIP

Printed in the United States of America

First Edition

1   2   3   4   5   6   7   8   9   10

BOOK DESIGN BY MICHAEL MENDELSOHN OF MM DESIGN 2000, INC.

CONTENTS

ACKNOWLEDGMENTS

For providing research information and aid for the preparation of this book we would like to thank the following organizations:

The California Governor's Office of Emergency Services (OES); Bay Area Regional Earthquake Preparedness Project (BAREPP); Underwriters Laboratories, Inc. (UL); National Fire Protection Association (NFPA); American Scald Burn Foundation (ASBF); the Federal Emergency Management Agency (FEMA) and the Residential Sprinkler Program of the U.S. Fire Administration; the Hennepin County (Minnesota) Medical Center (HCMC); Shriners Burns Institutes; Unicare Health Facilities, Inc.; National Oceanic and Atmospheric Administration (NOAA); and the National Child Safety Council.

INTRODUCTION

The year 1991 was a milestone. The U.S. suffered the lowest number of accidental deaths since 1924. The bad news was that in this record year the National Safety Council (800-621-7615) counted 88,000 deaths by accident. Of these fatalities, 43,500 were from automobile accidents.

Of the other 44,500 fatalities, 20,500 occurred in the home. Slips and falls killed 6,100 people; 4,900 died from poisoning. Fires and burns accounted for another 3,500 deaths; 2,400 people suffocated, and firearms were the cause of 800 accidental deaths. Drowning took a toll of 800 people, and 5,500 more died from a variety of other accidents. Dr. Daniel Della-Giustina, chairman of the Department of Safety Studies at West Virginia University, asserts that bad weather or pollution accounts for only about 5 percent of accidental deaths, with another 5 percent caused by faulty engineering. This means that upwards of 90 percent of all accidental deaths are caused by some sort of human error, and thus are preventable.

The accidental death toll does not tell the whole story. Tens of thousands of us suffer painful injuries, loss of work time and income, and millions of dollars in property losses, all resulting from emergencies that might have been prevented.

Not all home emergencies are life-threatening. Some are merely annoying, while others may be expensive but may not threaten our life or health. Still, statistics indicate that with routine maintenance and inspection of our property, and with some emergency planning, we may avoid most of these emergencies and may come through unavoidable emergencies with less strain both to temper and to our bank account.

CHAPTER ONE

125

CHILDPROOF YOUR HOME

TIPS

1 GARAGE DOORS

News accounts often report of young children being injured when the safety-reverse feature fails on a garage door opener. But, while it is true that these door openers may fail, it is also true that many injuries occur from contact with manual garage doors. For example, the Consumer Product Safety Commission (CPSC) reports that in 1992 there were 17,488 injuries caused by manual garage doors, and 3,063 reported injuries from doors having automatic garage door openers.

A manually operated garage door can close with great speed, especially if springs or other door hardware fail. Because one has hand contact with the door while opening or closing it, fingers or hands may be pinched between the panels of the door. When equipped with an opener, garage doors move more slowly and can be stopped at any point for safety. Also, automatic openers are activated by remote control, with the operator some distance away. Because the operator is not in contact with the door, fewer injuries can occur. The evidence is that having a garage door opener makes the home safer, but there still are hazards to watch for.

Don't let your child play with the garage door. Nearly 13,000 accidents occur annually when fingers or feet are injured in garage doors or hardware.

GARAGE DOOR OPENERS

2

Garage door openers can offer convenience as well as provide security. But they can also be a hazard, particularly for young children. Each year, young children are injured or killed when trapped under a garage door. Never permit children to play with the garage door opener, and never permit them to push the "close" button and try to run under the door before it closes. Automated garage door openers are required to have a safety-reverse feature. This feature causes the door to stop and reverse, or open, if it hits any obstacle while closing. But anything mechanical is subject to failure, and the stop-reverse feature may cease to work without any warning.

At least once a month, check the safety-reverse feature of your garage door opener to be sure it is working properly. Place a scrap of wood such as a 2 × 4 under the door's path, then push the close button. When the door's lower edge hits the 2 × 4 block, the opener should stop, reverse direction, and open within two seconds. If the opener fails to reverse direction when the door hits the 2 × 4, disconnect the opener and call a repairman.

Some new garage door operator controls, such as Stanley's Safe-T-Close System, include infrared units. This noncontact sensor stops and reverses the closing garage door if any object moves under the door and breaks the infrared beam. Mount the sensor unit on the wall near the floor, at either side of the garage door. If the infrared beam is broken by something moving under the door, the opener will reverse and raise the door. This unit is optional on all seven of Stanley's garage door openers. It is easy to install and provides inexpensive insurance for the young children in your home.

Garage door openers should stop automatically if the door hits any object before closing. Some types of sensors use an infrared beam to stop the door if an object blocks the door's path.

3 ELECTRICAL OUTLET COVERS

Small children have inquiring minds and are prone to investigate everything in sight. Unfortunately, this inquisitive nature can get them into trouble. One such potential source of danger lies in the slots in electrical outlets or receptacles into which children may push metal objects. To protect against electrical shock, buy and use plastic covers to guard every open or unused receptacle. The plastic disks are often sold in combination with foam plastic sealers. This combination of foam plastic sealers and plastic disks or air blockers not only saves energy by stopping air infiltration around the electrical outlets, it also serves as a safety barrier to probing fingers or metal implements. They cost only pennies each at home center stores.

In addition to covering unused electrical outlets, check power cords on appliances to prevent burns or electrical shock to children. Don't let power cords dangle where a child can pull on them. Try to hide them behind furniture—for example, run a lamp or radio cord behind a bed or end table—and avoid the use of extension cords with lamps or appliances. For cords that dangle below tables or countertops, fold up the excess cord footage and use twist ties to gather the excess cord into a neat bundle so there are no dangling loops to tempt children. Some heating appliances, such as coffee makers or toasters, can injure a child both by electrical shock and by burns if he pulls on dangling power cords and pulls the appliance down on himself.

Plastic covers prevent children from inserting objects into the receptacle and getting an electrical shock.

4 FIREARM SECURITY

If you are a hunter or keep firearms for home protection, there is a very real danger that the firearms may pose a hazard to other family members, particularly to small children who do not know how to handle them. When considering how to store your firearms safely, consider not only your own children, but also think about any grandchildren or visitors who may come into your home. There are two primary rules for firearm safety: Never bring a loaded firearm indoors, and always treat any firearm as though it were loaded. Other rules to observe are:

- If you keep firearms in your home, buy a locking gun cabinet and always lock all firearms away. And never leave the gun cabinet key "hidden" near the gun cabinet where it can easily be found by children or others.
- Equip each individual firearm with a trigger lock so any unauthorized person who gains entry to the cabinet still cannot discharge the firearm.
- Do not store ammunition in the same cabinet with the firearms.
- Treat all firearms as though they were loaded, and insist that anyone who handles them do the same. *Never point a firearm at anything you do not want to shoot.*
- Don't teach children gun safety yourself. Seek out state-approved firearm safety programs to train your youngsters or other family members in handling firearms.
- Never take an untrained novice afield. The excitement of the hunt or chase can cause even experienced hunters to make mistakes, and youngsters should never learn firearm safety while engaged in an actual hunting situation.

Don't keep a loaded gun where a child might find it. Never store a firearm and ammunition in the same place.

- Consider the maturity level and mental makeup of your family members before training them in the use of firearms. A person who is high-strung and becomes flighty under pressure is not a good candidate for handling firearms.
- If any member of your family has a problem with alcohol or other drugs, remove any firearms from the home and sell them, or store them else-where until the drug problem is resolved. Under no circumstances should you make firearms readily available to those whose judgment is obviously impaired, such as those under the influence of drugs.
- Never try to play Dirty Harry with an intruder. Material possessions are not worth dying—or killing—for. Resort to firearms only when family members fear for their lives.

5 POISON HAZARDS

Many chemicals and drugs that are commonly found around the household pose a real poison hazard to young children. For example, prescription drugs such as medicine for a cardiac condition, antidepressants, tranquilizers, or diuretics must be taken only in prescribed doses, because they may be toxic if taken as an overdose. But common over-the-counter drugs also are threats when taken improperly. Aspirin and related painkillers, vitamins, and ordinary iron tablets are all dangerous if taken improperly. Such everyday items as mouthwashes can have a minty taste and an attractive color, so they invite children to sample them. But the mouthwashes may contain as much as 30 percent alcohol and for a child can be harmful or even fatal if swallowed. Store these products in a childproof medicine cabinet or on upper shelves of a linen closet where they will be out of reach for small children. And avoid casual use of aspirin or other drugs for small children, because they will associate the drugs with being well and may overdose with them.

Don't leave household cleaning products or insecticides in lower cabinets or within the reach of small children. Inexpensive plastic child locks can be screwed to cabinet frames or doors to childproof cabinet doors and drawers. Most insect pests can be eliminated without the use of insecticides. For example, cockroaches must have food, water, and cracks to hide in if they are to survive in a given environment. Fix any leaking pipes, clean frequently to eliminate food crumbs, and caulk up cracks where the roaches can hide so

**Teach your child to recognize the
universal poison symbol: Mr. Yuk!**

there is no reason for them to stick around. If you must use insecticide products, at the least store them on high shelves, out of easy reach, or better still store them in a lockable shop or storage area.

House plants can liven up an interior, but if eaten, some, such as the berries from mistletoe, may cause illness and are thus not suited to homes where there are children. Check on their toxicity with your nursery before bringing new plants into the home.

If, despite your best preventive efforts, you have a poison emergency, call the emergency room or poison center at your local hospital, or call 911 and ask for medical help.

6 SMOKING

Smoking can be harmful to children in a variety of ways, not the least of which is teaching a bad habit to the child. But there is the further problem of leaving matches or lighters about where children might play with them and cause a fire. There are many cases on record of small children playing with a cigarette lighter and setting their own clothes or bedding on fire. Eliminate lighters and matches from children's reach.

Most important, however, is the direct health threat from cigarette smoke, both to smokers and to nonsmokers alike. Medical experts estimate that fully one third of all cancers could be prevented if we would simply stop smoking. According to the Environmental Protection Agency (EPA), "Published risk estimates place environmental tobacco smoke (ETS) among the most harmful indoor pollutants, and higher in risk than many environmental pollutants currently regulated by the EPA." Published medical reports point to new and mounting evidence that tobacco smoke is dangerous not only to the smokers but to everyone who inhales the smoke, especially for those such as children who are included in sensitive populations. For your own health and others', don't smoke. If you do smoke, do it outdoors, away from others.

In addition to tobacco smoke, the smoke from wood-burning stoves can be a hazard. Some medical experts have estimated that children living in homes where there is wood heat have double the incidence of bronchitis, colds, and other such respiratory distress. If you intend to have a wood-burning stove, be sure it is airtight. If you install a wood-burning fireplace, be sure that it has a fresh air duct to bring in outside combustion air, so that the smoke does not contaminate indoor air.

 # 7 COOKING STOVE DANGERS

It may be tempting to keep children in sight by letting them play on the kitchen floor while you are preparing meals, but it is a dangerous practice. When preparing meals, it is easy to drop or spill boiling pans of food or water, thereby burning a child. In yanking on a dangling electrical cord, a child may pull down a Crock-Pot, coffee maker, or electric fry pan, plus their contents, upon herself. For your own protection and to protect children, follow these kitchen safety rules:

- Don't leave cooking food unattended.
- Don't hang curtains or store anything above a stove.
- Turn pot handles inward, over the cooktop, so they do not protrude over its edges. Pot and pan handles that extend over cooktop edges may be bumped, or children may reach up and pull them down upon themselves.
- Don't leave pot holders on the stove or cooktop, where they may start fire.
- Don't wear loose-fitting or baggy clothes while cooking.
- Don't pour water on a grease fire. Instead, slide a lid over the pan to smother the flames and turn off the burner.

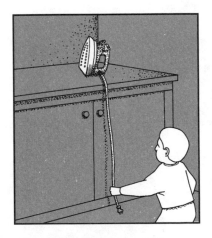

Always store electric appliances out of children's reach. Dangling electrical cords are irresistible playthings to young children, and small appliances should be stored away immediately after use.

To prevent burns, turn the handles on pots and pans inward, over the cooktop. Handles that extend over the edge can be accidentally bumped, spilling the hot contents.

8 TOOLS

Tools are intended to hammer, cut, or abrade whatever they come into contact with; unfortunately, this may include human skin. Teach children from the crawling stage onward that tools are not playthings and should be left alone. Keep household tools in a locked toolbox, or behind the locked doors of a shop. Keep sharp tools such as chisels in their own wooden storage boxes (unlike metal boxes, wooden tool boxes absorb moisture and help protect the tools from rusting). Buy plastic blade guards for handsaws, or make your own guard by cutting a saw kerf or slot into a scrap of wood that is as long as the saw blade. Secure the blade guard to the saw blade via heavy-duty rubber bands.

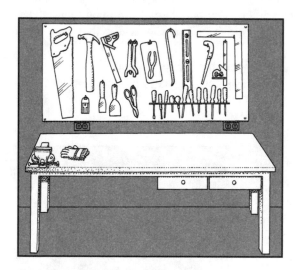

Store hand tools in a designated shop area, out of the reach of children.

9 POWER TOOLS

Power tools require that particular precautions be taken.

- To keep out intruders, install a door and lock on the home shop, and don't leave the key where it can be found.
- Disconnect extension cords and tool power cords so the tools must be plugged in before they can be operated.
- When setting up a workshop, add a separate control panel with a master switch so that you can turn off power to all shop outlets with one switch.
- Remove drill bits or other accessories from drills when you have finished using them.
- Do not remove safety features such as trigger locks or blade guards from power tools.
- Keep children and others out of the shop while you are operating power tools. Movement and conversation by others can be distracting to the tool operator.

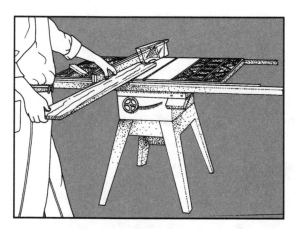

Observe safety warnings and keep protective guards in place when using power tools. Disconnect power tools when not in use.

10 DROWNING

Most children who drown are left unattended in or near water while the parent or other sitter is momentarily distracted. The greatest danger is to young children who are large enough to move about, but not strong enough to find their way out of a dangerous situation. The first rule of child protection is never to leave toddlers unattended in the bath or near obvious possible water hazards, such as wading or swimming pools. Remember, too, that your swimming or wading pool may be legally considered to be an "attractive nuisance," i.e., a structure that at the same time may attract and endanger children. This means that you must not only take steps to protect your own children from water hazards but also that you must erect fences or other barriers to keep out neighbor children. Remember also that a child who is too small to understand the principle of boundaries cannot be considered to be trespassing, so the burden is on the homeowner to protect children who wander onto his property.

Perhaps more dangerous are the less obvious drowning hazards. For example, because they are so commonly available, 5-gallon plastic pails have become very popular for use in the garden or for scrub pails for washing the car. It is reported that in the past 5 years 125 children have drowned from falling into 5-gallon plastic pails. Small toddlers often reach for the water or sponge in the pail, tumble forward, and drown when they cannot free themselves from the pails. Most vulnerable are children in the 8- to 14-month age range. Keep children away while using the 5-gallon pails for chores that involve carrying water, or switch to a smaller plastic scrub pail that will not pose a hazard to children.

Even the common 5-gallon pail may be a risk for young children. They may drink the contents or climb or fall in and drown.

11 BURNS, SCALDING

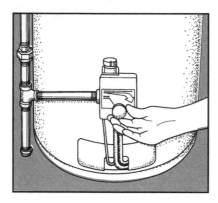

To prevent scald burns from hot water, turn down the water heater thermostat to no more than 120 degrees Fahrenheit.

While visiting others' bathrooms, have you ever been burned by hot water from a lavatory faucet? Then it is easy to understand the horror stories in the news describing the hot water burn injuries or deaths of small children who play with water faucets. While it is always advisable to test the bathwater temperature before you place a child in the tub, remember that a child may play with a hot water faucet in your absence, and the child will not mix hot and cold water to reach a comfortable temperature level. It is much safer to turn down the water heater thermostat so the water temperature is cool enough that it cannot burn a child.

If your house has a dishwasher, the plumber may have set your water heater thermostat at 140 degrees Fahrenheit. This is an acceptable temperature if all members of the family are old enough to mix cold water with hot water when running a bath, but water drawn straight from the hot water faucet may burn a child. When selecting a thermostat setting for your water heater, remember that a child's skin is more tender than an adult's skin, so what is comfortable for you may be too hot for a child. Both the American Red Cross and the American Academy of Pediatrics recommend that the water heater thermostat be set so the water is no hotter than 120 degrees Fahrenheit. While a child's skin may redden from exposure to water of this temperature, serious burns will not develop.

If you have a burn injury, check to determine how serious the burn is. If skin is red, mottled, or has closed blisters, the burn may be first- or second-degree. Immerse the burn in cold (not ice) water, or apply a cold compress such as a wet towel to the burn area. If the burn is second-degree with open blisters or third-degree with white or charred skin, cover with a clean cloth or sheet to keep the affected area clean. Then seek medical attention.

12 CRIB SAFETY

Crib accidents for babies once totaled up to 50,000 injuries and 200 deaths per year, but the federal government mandated safety standards for cribs in 1973. Today's cribs are far safer because of those tougher standards. But if you are using a relative's hand-me-down crib, or are budget-shopping garage sales, it pays to try to find out when the crib was made and to take your measuring tape along. First, if a crib is more than 15 years old (built in 1978 or before) it's a good idea to pass it by. Many cribs made prior to 1978 are coated with lead-based paint that is toxic to children. If the crib was made after 1978, the finish should be lead-free.

Next, check the hardware on the crib. Set the bed up and shake it from end to end and from side to side to be sure hardware is in place and undamaged. Check for loose screws or bolts that might fail and cause a problem. Pay particular attention to the hardware brackets that support the springs and mattress.

Now check the crib slats to be sure none are cracked or broken. Measure the distance between crib slats. The accepted maximum distance between slats is 2½ inches. Wider slat spacing may permit the child's body, but not its head, to slip between the slats. The child then can strangle or choke, a common accident in older cribs.

Now position the crib mattress at its highest setting with the adjustable or dropside down. The top of the dropside should be at least 9 inches above the top of the mattress support so an infant cannot roll out of the crib. Now position the dropside in the fully up position, and the mattress support at its lowest setting. Measure the distance from the top of the mattress support to the top of the raised dropside. To prevent an older child from climbing out, the distance should be at least 26 inches.

Check the fit of the mattress to the sides of the crib. Try to insert two fingers all along the gap around the mattress perimeter. If the fit is loose, the child's face may become trapped in the gap, and suffocation could result.

Cribs are available in single or double dropside models, so the parent can lower either or both sides to take care of the child. Check the dropside releases and hardware on either or both sides to be sure a small child cannot release the sides.

Check the crib for corner posts that protrude above the side rails, or for decorative doodads or cutouts. Any object that protrudes from the crib frame may snag a baby's clothes or cause other injury.

13 CHILDREN AND LEAD POISONING

Because children play or crawl on the floors and are prone to put things in their mouths, they are especially at risk from lead poisoning. It is estimated that three fourths of houses built before 1978 have lead paint. If you live in an older house or apartment, have the space checked for lead contamination. This contamination may involve lead in wall or ceiling paint, lead-based paint on older furniture, lead in drinking water (usually from lead solder in water pipes), and lead in the lawn or garden soil (from lead in regular gasoline— now prohibited—which after being burned, is deposited there by air), or from lead-based exterior house paint. To minimize lead poisoning dangers to children, always supervise them when they are playing outdoors. Don't let a child put dirt in his mouth. Buy or build a sandbox, fill it with clean sand, and teach the child to play in the sand, not in the dirt.

Indoors, put a fresh coat of lead-free paint on ceilings, walls, and woodwork. Position the child's crib or bed far enough from walls or woodwork that the child cannot reach paint chips or put his mouth on window sills or other painted surfaces. Keep the child's bed or crib free of paint chips. Wipe down windowsills and base trim, and mop floors frequently to pick up any paint particles that may contain lead.

If you have older furniture such as chairs or dressers in children's rooms, paint them with a fresh coat of lead-free paint. Don't sand or use a heat gun to remove old paint, because you may release lead dust into the air. Instead, wipe the old paint with a liquid sander to prepare it for the new paint coat. Liquid sander products are available at any paint store. Replace older cribs or beds with new models, because a child may chew on lead-painted surfaces of older cribs (see Crib Safety, p. 17).

If you think there may be lead-based paint in your living area, don't let a child play on the floor. The floors may be covered with paint chips or dust that can contain lead. Buy the child a playpen and keep him in it. Remove rugs or carpets from areas where there is lead paint; wood floors are easier to clean than carpeted floors.

Children and pregnant women are especially at risk from exposure to lead. Buy bottled water for cooking and for children to drink. To avoid possible lead poisoning from tap water, use bottled water to make any baby formula. Keep in mind that lead-free solder is now used in water pipes in newer houses, and the greatest danger of lead poisoning is to those living in houses built before 1978. For answers to specific questions, call the National Lead Information Center at 800-LEAD-FYI.

18

14 LEARNING ABOUT MATCHES

Fire experts suggest that when it comes to matches or cigarette lighters, the rule should be "no touch" for any child who is under five years of age. But from about age five, children should be taught the proper function and safe use of matches. The experts point out that the earlier the child learns the proper and safe use of fire, the less likely is the desire to play with matches and fire.

How can a parent teach a child about matches while at the same time avoiding a fire tragedy? Experts advise that rather than making the negative statement "Don't play with matches," the parents instead teach the child that fire and matches are tools to be used for positive purposes such as cooking our food or heating our homes. We should also teach that fire that is improperly used can cause pain, death, and destruction. A list of suggestions from the Shriners Burns Institute follows:

- Teach children that fire is a tool to be used by adults, not a toy for children.
- Never keep kitchen or "strike anywhere" matches in the house where young children are present. Keep only safety matches in the house.
- Keep all matches and cigarette lighters out of the reach of young children, especially those under five.
- Teach children under five years of age that they should go tell an adult if they find matches or a cigarette lighter, rather than bringing the matches or lighter to the adult.
- Avoid using a cigarette lighter as a "spark toy" to amuse a small child.
- Try to minimize the child's curiosity by demonstrating the useful purposes of a match such as lighting a candle, a campfire, or a fireplace.
- Teach the child how to light a match. Steps include:

  1. Open the package (match folder) and remove the match.
  2. Close the package and turn it over to the striking side.
  3. Hold the match in the proper position and strike it away from the body.
  4. After ignition, hold the match in a horizontal position for 2–3 seconds.
  5. Blow out the flame and let the match cool to the touch (5–10 seconds).

- Satisfy the child's curiosity. Following the above steps, let the child strike matches repeatedly, as many as he wants, until he tires of the action.

19

- Tell the child that in the future she can light matches and use fire only in the presence of an adult, under safe conditions.
- Be sure all adults in the house set a good example in using fire and matches.
- By developing and practicing a home fire escape plan, and by installing smoke detectors in the house, we encourage fire safety awareness. Give a child responsibilities in home fire safety to encourage a positive attitude toward fire.

15 MISSING CHILDREN

A growing and frightening threat to children is the threat of abduction. Thousands of children disappear every year. To help you protect your children, the National Child Safety Council (517-764-6070 in Jackson, Mississippi) has put together a list of steps to instruct the child. Try to teach a child to be wary, without causing undue alarm or stress. Emphasize that the instructions are intended to help the child in case of emergency.

- Teach the child your full address, area code, and phone number. Also, teach him to dial your home phone number, and how to dial 911 or zero for operator to get help in an emergency.
- Keep an identification file on your child. The file should include a current photo and description, including any identifying features such as birthmarks or surgical scars.
- Take time to check the child's clothes each morning, so you will know what she is wearing that day.
- A stranger may gain a child's confidence if he calls the child by name, so don't display your child's name where it is visible on books or clothes. To mark ownership, write the child's name inside the book cover and on the inside of articles of clothing.
- Teach the child how to find you if you two become separated in a crowded store. Emphasize that the child should not begin to wander aimlessly looking for you, but should go immediately to a checkout counter or store clerk (for example, the one wearing the name tag, or red shirt) and ask for help.
- Have your local police department take a set of your child's fingerprints or footprints so absolute identification is possible.
- Ask the school to call you if your child is absent. Even better, ask the school to adopt a policy requiring that all parents be called to confirm that their child's absence is legitimate.
- Advise the child's school or day-care center who will pick up the child each day. Try to have the same person (father, mother, baby-sitter) pick up the child at school each day, and instruct the child and his teacher that he is to leave only with the authorized person.
- Teach the child that some bad persons may use tricks to get a child to go with them. Point out examples, such as offering a child candy or other treats, telling the child that the abductor is acting for the child's mother, or suggesting that the child go with the abductor to a "fun" place or event.

Teach the child never to go to a stranger or to a strange vehicle, but if approached quickly to move away and go to a place of safety.

- Walk with the child to school or the playground, and set boundaries where the child should not go, for example, into alleys or vacant lots. Tell the child what to do if a stranger approaches him, and to move away from anyone who appears to be following him.

- Organize a neighborhood "safe house" program to establish and mark safe houses where occupants will be home and will aid a child who asks for help.

MISSING

Melissa Ann Collins   **Jasmine Kirlissa Collins**

Date Missing: 08/08/91	Date Missing: 08/08/91
From: Akron, OH	From: Akron, OH
Age: 19 years	Age: 2 years
DOB: 11/25/73	DOB: 12/29/90
BLACK FEMALE	BLACK FEMALE
Eyes: Brown	Eyes: Brown
Hair: Brown	Hair: Black
Height: 5' 3"	Height: 1' 6"
Weight: 120 lbs.	Weight: 12-17 lbs.

If you can identify this child or any other missing child, report all information you may have to The National Center for Missing and Exploited Children:

1-800-843-5678

Follow the tips above to protect your child. For emergency use, have a current photo and full biographic information sheet prepared for each child.

CHAPTER TWO

125

STAIRS, STEPS, FALLS

TIPS

16 SECURE HANDRAILS

As you move on stairs, the handrail can be a useful aid to help you keep your balance, but to protect you from injury in case of a fall any handrail should be strong enough, and securely anchored enough, to support an adult's weight.

Unfortunately, the hardware or brackets of many residential handrails are anchored with wood screws that are too short to hold an adult's full weight. If the handrail pulls free from the wall under your weight, it will be of little help when you fall.

There are two basic handrail types. The first type is fastened directly to a wall via brackets. The second type is the freestanding handrail or balustrade, seen on the open side of a stairway. A handrail is required only on one side of stairways that are less than 44 inches wide. Building codes state that handrail height should be at least 30 inches, but not more than 36 inches, above the treads. Standard handrail diameter is 1⅝ inches, large enough to support an adult's weight but small enough that the hand can completely encircle the rail and grip it securely.

A freestanding handrail or balustrade is secured in place by newel posts and balusters. The post at the bottom of a staircase is called a starting newel post, and the post at the top or landing of the staircase is called a landing newel post. The balusters support the handrail between the two newel posts. If the handrail is loose from the balusters, or balusters and/or newel posts are loose at the base, the repairs are beyond the ability of the average person,

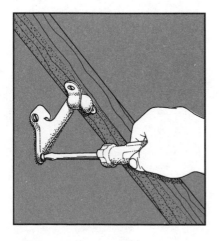

To ensure that a handrail can support your weight, check the bracket screws. If necessary, replace them with longer screws.

and a professional carpenter should be called to reinforce or tighten all the components of the staircase.

If the stairs have a wall-mounted handrail, check the spacing between the handrail supports or brackets. The brackets should be spaced no more than four feet apart, and should be located so that bracket screws go into solid wood wall studs or other framing. Check the brackets for loose or missing screws. Use a screwdriver to remove a couple of the bracket screws and check their length. The screws holding the rail must pass through the bracket base and the plaster or wallboard, or a total of ¾ inch to 1 inch of material, before they reach the studs. This may mean that the screws must be 2 inches long in order to properly penetrate the solid wood base. If the bracket screws do not penetrate at least 1 inch into the wood studs, replace them with longer screws.

17 STAIR MATH

When building, remodeling, or adding a porch or deck, be sure any new stairs or steps are built with safety in mind. This means that you figure the stair math carefully. Try to maintain at least 6 feet 8 inches of head room above the stairs. This height prevents any head bumping, plus it allows space for moving large furniture or other items up or down stairs more easily. Build stairs so that the angle between the stair carriage and the floor is 30 to 35 degrees. This stair angle will ensure climbing ease while taking up only a minimum of floor space.

There is a rhythm to climbing stairs, and any interruption in this rhythm can result in a dangerous fall. For example, if stair risers or perpendicular boards between steps are 7 inches high, with an odd 8-inch-high riser at the end, the higher riser will present a tripping hazard, because the climber has set a climbing rhythm to raise the foot only so far. Stair risers should be laid out so they are all equal. Divide the height of the staircase by the number of risers so they all are equally spaced.

Another safety factor is the width of the stair tread. Stair tread width should be wide enough so that the foot is totally supported by the tread. A basic rule is that minimum tread width should be equal to 24 inches, minus 2 × riser height. In addition, maximum tread width should be equal to 25 inches, minus 2 × riser height. Thus, if the riser height is 7 inches, the tread should be 24 − 14 = 10 inches (minimum), or 25 − 14 = 11 inches (maximum) wide. Again, a tread width that is too narrow can let the foot slip and cause a fall; a tread width that is too wide can interfere with a normal stride and again cause a trip-and-fall accident.

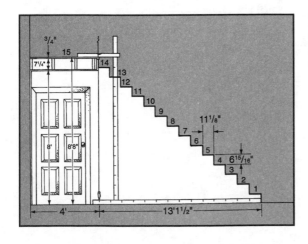

For future stair safety observe proper dimensions for tread width and spacing.

18 STAIR SAFETY

Many stair accidents occur because the stairway is dark, visibility is poor, and the climber misjudges where the steps end. Install lighting so that steps are clearly lit and defined, and the edge of each step can be seen. For maximum traction consider using a slip-proof paint or clear polyurethane floor finish on stair treads. If you choose to carpet the treads, select a firm, thin pad and tightly woven carpet for stair treads. Thick padding or carpet will interfere with safe footing, and the combined bulk of carpet and pad on the riser face will reduce the usable width of the tread.

Toys left lying about can cause dangerous falls. Teach children to keep stairs free of toys and all other clutter. An inspection of many basement stairs may reveal bowling balls, brooms and mops, vacuum cleaner hoses, and a case of canned beverage "stored" on the steps. Do not store shoes, clothes, stacks of old newspapers, cleaning tools, supplies, or canned food or beverages on basement stairs. Any item left on stairs reduces the usable width and area of tread and greatly increases the chance of a nasty fall.

Stair treads should be kept well lighted, free of clutter. For safety, handrail should end exactly even with last step or landing so people can judge end of staircase.

19 DECK INSPECTION

Most of us assume that our deck is well built, securely anchored to the house, and adequately supported by posts. But, a summer rarely passes without news of a deck collapsing because of structural faults. It is wise to inspect the underside of a deck each spring, before summer use begins, to be sure the deck is in good shape. Following is a list of things to look for when inspecting the structure of a wood deck. If you do not trust your own judgment, hire a contractor or building inspector to check the deck for you.

First, check the deck construction to be sure that proper carpentry procedures were observed. For example, bright steel nails should not be used for building exterior projects. To avoid rust, all fasteners (nails or deck screws) should be either hot-dipped galvanized, aluminum, or stainless steel. The ledger joist, or the joist that is parallel to, and attached to, the house, should have spacers to provide a slight gap between itself and the house rim joist or siding. If the wood members are nailed or bolted together with no gap, water can be trapped between the two members and premature rot can occur. There should also be a slight gap of perhaps ⅛ inch between the deck boards. This gap permits rain to drain between the boards so the deck lumber can dry and avoid wood rot.

Try to determine what species of wood was used to build the deck. Because of their durability and resistance to rot, cedar, redwood, or pressure-treated lumber are preferred for deck construction. If less durable woods such as untreated pine or spruce were used in the deck, wood rot may cause the deck structure to fail.

Use a sharp knife or carpenter's awl to probe the ledger joist, the joist that secures the deck structure to the house, for signs of wood rot. If the wood is soft and the probe can be pushed easily into the wood, there may be wood rot in the joist. Proceed with the awl to check the wood joists, steps and stair stringers, deck boards, and support posts. Any wood joint is subject to water entry and rot. Probe carefully at joints where posts and joists meet. If any wood rot is found, you must replace the rotted framing member; call in a building contractor to inspect the deck and suggest what repairs are needed if rot seems widespread. While under the deck, check the joists and bridging for any signs of joists twisting. Joists will support the greatest load when they are perfectly perpendicular to the posts or beams they rest upon. A twisted joist may slip and collapse completely. Hire a carpenter to pry twisted joists back into position, and install solid bridging to hold them from future twisting.

Check all deck support hardware, such as metal joist or step hangers. If these metal connectors seem loose, renail them; if they are still sound but rusted, sand off as much rust as possible, prime the metal with a primer made for rusty metal, then paint with an exterior metal paint.

Check to be sure the deck railing is free of rot and securely fastened. Renail or tighten nails and lag screws as needed. Check to be sure that rail balusters are spaced so that no child can push his head between them.

Finally, when inviting guests onto any deck that is above ground level, use proper judgment. Like any structure, decks are built with a reasonable load limit, and dancing or other vigorous activity may tax the deck's load limit.

Use a carpenter's awl or ice pick to test for dry rot of deck framing. Drive popped nails or loose screws.

20 ICY STEPS, WALKS

In states with winter snowfall, city ordinances often make the homeowner responsible for shoveling the public walk in front of his property. So, icy steps or walks can not only be a hazard to your own family, but can also cause you to be sued for negligence if a visitor is injured by a fall. For safety's sake, keep walks free of ice in winter, and keep them free of clutter or debris year-round.

To keep walks and steps free of ice, shovel them immediately after a snowfall. Foot traffic will compact the snow and make removal difficult. The sun will also glaze snow with an icy crust. If the snow is removed before it turns to ice, the sun's rays will soon dry the walk or steps. Icy patches can be removed with a commercial ice remover product.

One key to ice-free walks and steps is to provide good drainage so rain or snow melt cannot run and puddle on or near the walkways. Standing water will freeze in cold weather, so take steps to provide water runoff. Dig shallow drainage ditches along the affected walk, or remove dirt to redirect the water away from the walk. Sagging or uneven concrete slabs can be raised into position by a system called concrete raising or mud jacking. Look for this service in the Yellow Pages under "Concrete Contractors."

Because most driveways and walks slope directly from the house to the storm gutters at the street, rain gutter installers often direct downspouts so they deposit water directly on a driveway or walk. This provides good drainage in warm weather, but during cold weather the water can freeze on the slabs. Survey gutter downspout placement to see whether water can be redirected away from the concrete slabs in cold weather.

To avoid falls keep steps free of ice and snow. Use commercial deicer to melt ice or freezing rain.

21 CARPET, SCATTER RUGS

When placed randomly on polished wood or vinyl floors, area or scatter rugs can cause painful and dangerous falls. Eliminate area rugs in such high-traffic and dangerous areas as the bottom of stairs or stair landings, and on tile, slate, or marble floors at entry doors. If you insist on having area rugs, be sure they have nonslip backing material. Rubber jar (canning) rings sewn to the back of rugs can help make them nonslip.

High-pile carpet can present a tripping hazard to the elderly or to anyone who uses a walker, cane, or crutches. The thick pile may tangle with toes or heels, or may snag a cane or a crutch tip. For the same reasons, any extra-thick padding can be a tripping hazard to anyone who is unsure afoot. For carpet safety buy a six-pound rebond (plastic foam) pad and a carpet with a short or tight-loop pile. New carpet should be stretched until it is tight and wrinkle-free. This not only extends the life of the carpet, but also avoids wrinkles that can catch a foot and trip up someone. When carpet layers install carpet, they may fail to take all the "stretch" out of it. This is a particular problem when installing very heavy carpet, because the thicker pile is very stiff and difficult to stretch. But after the carpet has been in place for a short time, the heavy carpet will "relax" and wrinkles can develop. Those wrinkles present a serious trip danger to those who walk across the carpet. The remedy is to ask the carpet layer to return after thirty to sixty days (when wrinkles develop) to restretch the carpet and eliminate the wrinkles.

Avoid using scatter or throw rugs on stair landings. Be sure any rugs placed on slippery floors have slip-proof backing.

22 EXTENSION CORDS

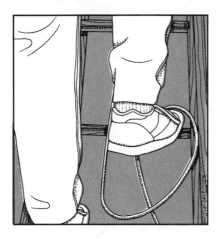

Route extension cords off a leg or rung of a ladder to avoid mishaps. Better yet, use cordless tools to accomplish repairs.

Electrical extension cords not only present a tripping hazard when run across the floors, but can also prove a fire hazard if the cords are run beneath rugs or carpets. To minimize the need for extension cords, electrical code standards dictate that modern houses must have an electrical outlet box every twelve feet. If your house has too few outlets, so that you must use extension cords for lamps or appliances, consider having an electrical contractor install extra outlets to bring the service up to code.

Don't let excess appliance power cord wire hang from kitchen cabinets or clutter the floor. Fold the excess cord wire into a neat bundle and use wire or plastic twist ties to hold the wires in a bundle. When neatly bundled, the excess wire cannot trip people or hang loose from cabinets, where inquisitive youngsters can tug on the cords and pull down the appliances.

When strung across the floor, attic, or roof deck, extension cords for power tools can present a real trip hazard. Extension cords are especially dangerous when carried up or down a ladder. The cords can become tangled around a worker's feet and cause a nasty spill. If you must use an extension cord while working on a ladder, route the cord off one rail or leg of the ladder, rather than hanging it over the ladder rungs where it might trip you up.

A better solution, where possible, is to buy and use cordless power tools for ladder or scaffold work. Using cordless tools eliminates both the danger of electrical shock and the danger of tripping over the power or extension cord. Not all power tools are available in cordless models, so learn to keep extension cords out of the walking or climbing path.

23 LADDER SAFETY

The U.S. Consumer Products Safety Commission (CPSC) reports that in the year 1989, 97,000 patients were treated at hospitals for ladder accidents. To avoid becoming another statistic, learn to choose and use ladders safety.

First, consider your own health and ability to climb ladders. If the exertion taxes you or you are afraid of heights, leave the ladder work to pros.

When buying a ladder, be aware of the duty rating or weight capacity that is listed on the ladder label. Don't buy on price alone. Ladders vary in cost, and are rated for their weight capacity. When shopping, remember to consider not only your own weight, but the weight of tools and materials you must move up the ladder. A Type III ladder is a lightweight household ladder designed to hold 200 pounds. A Type II ladder will hold 225 pounds, and a Type I ladder will support 250 pounds. If your own body weight is 200 pounds or more, consider buying a commercial Type IA ladder, which will support 300 pounds. This will ensure that you can safely climb the ladder while carrying a heavy weight, such as a bundle of roofing shingles.

Never use a chair for climbing. Buy a proper step stool or ladder. Read and observe the ladder warning labels. On stepladders, spread the legs completely apart and lock the folding braces into place. Do not use the top step or fold-out tray of the ladder as a step. Don't paint wood ladders. Paint can

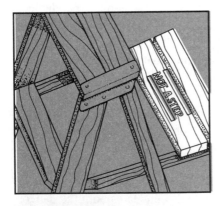

Read and heed all label warnings printed on any stepladder, particularly the caution against using the tray shelf as a step.

Periodically check the step brace nuts to make sure they are tight. If not, tighten each securely with an adjustable wrench.

conceal cracks in the ladder legs or steps. Inspect the ladder frequently to be sure everything is in good shape. Use a wrench to tighten any hardware nuts on steps or braces.

For extension ladders, be sure to position the legs on firm soil. If the ladder is placed on wet soil, a leg may sink into the soil, tipping the ladder to one side and spilling the worker. Place the bottom of the ladder about one quarter of its length from the house wall; i.e., when using a 16-foot ladder, the bottom of the ladder should be about 4 feet from the house. Do not lean or reach to the side of a ladder. Use both hands to climb and keep your body positioned between the legs. When using a metal ladder, be careful to keep it away from electrical power lines.

24 EXERCISE EQUIPMENT

Sales of home exercise equipment have contributed significantly to the growth and maturation of the weight-loss industry. As we have become more active, exercise-related injuries have also increased. Accidental injuries incurred in the use of exercise equipment result in 25,000 emergency room visits a year. When misused, stair climbers, weights and weight machines, bikes, treadmills, and ski and rowing machines may all pose hazards.

Before starting a home exercise program, consult your own physician. He or she can advise whether your health dictates any limits on prudent exercise. Don't overdo, and stick with a regimen designed for your age and physical condition. When shopping for exercise equipment, don't shop for price alone. Bargain equipment may be poorly built, so that springs, treads or other parts of the equipment can break or come loose and injure the operator. If you are not familiar with exercise equipment, ask an aerobic instructor or knowledgeable salesperson to assist you in your selection. Choose only equipment that is sturdy and well built.

Failure to read and follow the manufacturer's instructions may result in more injuries than faulty exercise equipment does. If some home assembly is required, read and understand the instructions before attempting to assemble the equipment. Read instructions also for proper use, note any manufacturer's warnings, and be sure all family members are familiar with the rules for safe operation before letting them use the equipment.

25 BATHTUBS

When you consider how slick surfaces of fiberglass or porcelain tubs and showers are made more slippery by water and substances such as bath soap and shampoo, it should be no surprise that the bathroom is one of the most dangerous places in the home. To make the tub or shower floor more slip-proof, manufacturers frequently spray a textured finish on the surface of the tub floors, and we are all familiar with the peel-and-stick decorative items that can be stuck to the bathtub floor to improve a bather's footing. The most common and perhaps the most effective add-on item for slip-proofing the tub may be the rubber mats that can be attached to the tub floor with suction cups on the back side of the mat.

Bathtub falls are not caused only by the slippery-when-wet conditions. Not only is the footing poor, but in the average bath the walls of the tub or shower enclosure, being either fiberglass or ceramic tile, are also smooth and slippery. When one slips there is nothing to grab onto, and if one completes the fall he may find a not-so-comfortable and dangerous headrest of protruding steel water pipes.

To help accident-proof the bathroom, make the floors more slip-proof and install handrails, called grab bars, both to aid bathers in climbing in or out of the enclosure and to provide support if they lose their balance. Grab rails can be anchored to the walls, or can be attached as add-on items to the front edge of the bathtub. If you install the wall-mounted grab rails, be sure that the screws are anchored into wood studs or framing. Grab rails are available at any hospital supply store or from your plumbing contractor.

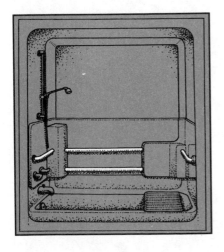

To help accident-proof the bathroom, install grab bars to aid in getting in/out of the tub or shower.

CHAPTER THREE

125

WATER PROBLEMS

TIPS

26 LEAKING ROOF

From a standpoint of total monetary loss, few home problems can cause so much damage as a leaking roof. Wet insulation, shorted electrical fixtures, damaged wallboard or plaster, and soaked furniture and accessories all add to the total loss caused by a roof leak, so it pays to keep the roof in good repair.

To prevent roof leaks, monitor the roof as it ages. If you do not feel safe climbing onto a roof, use a pair of binoculars to look for missing, windblown, or cracked shingles. As a roof ages, the sun dries out the shingles, and the protective surface granules begin to break away. Look into roof gutters or under gutter downspouts for excess granule deposits, a sure sign of failing roof shingles. Check for cracks in any area where there is a penetration of the roof deck, such as cutouts for vents, chimneys, or plumbing stacks. Look also at any valleys or flashing where the roof plane is broken, such as where a gable roof is interrupted by a dormer. Roof mastic for sealing cracks is available in caulk tubes. Apply a bead of roof mastic along the edge of flashings to seal small leaks.

Any roof that is more than 10 years old probably carried a warranty period of 15 to 20 years. If the roof was installed in the past decade, the shingles may have a warranty period of 20 to 30 years or more. Check the age and warranty period of your roof shingles. If the shingles are approaching the limits of the warranty period, it may be time for total roof replacement. If the roof appears to be somewhat aged but you are unsure whether it should be replaced, have the roof inspected by a professional. Also, check whether there is one layer or two layers of shingles on the roof. If the roof has only one layer of shingles, you can have another layer of shingles applied over the first. If the roof already has two layers of shingles, the old shingles must be removed and a new roof applied over the roof sheathing.

27 ROOF STORM DAMAGE

Hurricane Andrew and other recent megastorms have caused widespread roof damage. It comes as no surprise that winds of 170-mph velocity can raise havoc with asphalt roof shingles. But it has been shown that shingles applied with hot-dipped galvanized roofing nails were much less prone to wind damage than shingles that were stapled on with an air-powered stapler.

If you are planning on reshingling, you can take steps to make the roof more wind-resistant. If you are starting from scratch with the roof sheathing, the first line of defense against leaks will be an underlayment course of 15-pound felt covering the roof sheathing. Rather than use a staple gun, use metal washers or disks and galvanized nails to secure the felt. This will make the felt underlayment much more resistant to wind damage from storms. For best wind resistance, select shingles with self-sealing adhesive strips or individual lock-down shingles. The self-sealing shingles have strips of shingle adhesive covered with a protective strip that is removed when the shingles are installed. The heat of the sun on the roof will activate the adhesive, glue the two shingles together, and help lock down the shingle tabs. To install the asphalt shingles, use a carpenter's hammer or shingle hatchet and galvanized roofing nails. If you are installing a second layer of asphalt shingles over an existing layer, remember that you must use longer roofing nails in order to penetrate through the first or extra layer of shingles. Your roofing dealer can help you select the proper shingles, nails, and underlayment for your roof.

The above tips will help you build a roof that will withstand major windstorms. If you live in an area where high winds or windstorms are common,

If the roof leaks but the shingles are not wind damaged, suspect roof penetrations such as furnace stack, attic vents, or draining vents as likely sources.

you may suffer wind damage to the roof in spite of your best construction efforts. If you live in a storm area, keep a roll of 6-mil plastic or a large plastic tarp (drop cloth) handy to temporarily cover the roof in case of wind damage. You should buy and store the plastic covering before you actually have roof damage and need it. Because of the increase in demand, emergency repair materials are difficult to find after the storm has already done widespread damage.

28 WATER DAMAGE TO CEILINGS

If roof damage has occurred, the rain that falls on the roof will run into the attic and pool or puddle on the attic side of the ceilings. Water that runs quickly off the plaster or wallboard will do little damage to ceilings, but if water pools and soaks into plaster or wallboard the water will destroy the binder that holds the plaster (or plaster core of the wallboard) together, and the soaked area will turn soft and fail. If the water is allowed to stand and soak on the ceilings, widespread and expensive damage can occur.

Drill holes in the ceiling to minimize water damage. The small drain holes are much easier to repair than the wide damage that may result from standing water. After the water is removed and the roof repaired, you can use Spackle or plaster to patch the small drain holes.

To minimize or eliminate water damage to the plaster or wallboard, go into the attic, pull the insulation back, and check the topside of the ceilings to see where water is standing in puddles. If the water has been standing long, you will be able to see wet spots on the ceilings from the finished side. The trick is to remove the water as quickly as possible. To do this you must make a small drain hole in the ceiling to let the water run through. To avoid electric shock from water contact, use a cordless drill and ¼-inch bit to make the drain hole in the ceiling and let the water run through. Or use a 16 penny nail and hammer to make a hole in the ceiling material, then pull the nail out and let the water drain. If the water puddle covers a wide area on the ceiling, you may have to make multiple drain holes.

A wet spot indicates that water is standing on the ceiling. Use a cordless drill to make drain holes in a waterlogged plaster or drywall ceiling. Make sure to have a bucket handy to catch any water that is released.

29 WATER STAINS, CEILING

If water stands and soaks on the attic side of the ceiling, water stains may develop on the finished ceiling (plaster or wallboard). If you attempt to paint over the water stains using latex paint, the water in the paint may activate them and cause them to bleed through the new paint coat. If you attempt to cover the stains with a second coat—even a third or fourth coat—of latex paint, the stains will continue to bleed through the paint coats. To seal the stains so they cannot bleed through your paint, apply a coat of fast-drying sealer over the stain area. Fast-drying sealers are available with trade names such as BIN or KILZ.

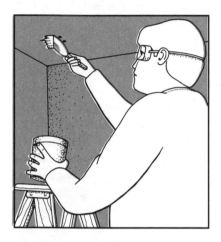

Once the ceiling has been allowed to dry and the source of the leak repaired, apply Spackle with a flexible putty knife to fill in the drainage holes. A severely stained ceiling will have to be sanded and primed before repainting.

30 WET ATTIC INSULATION

One of the immediate problems from a roof leak is that attic insulation may be soaked. Obviously, the soggy wet insulation will retain moisture, and the wet insulation not only is less efficient than dry, but the trapped moisture also can cause mildew, mold, odors, and soak damage to the plaster or wallboard ceiling. So, after getting the roof fixed and the leak stopped, the next problem is to dry out the insulation.

The water from the roof leak will obviously flow to the bottom of the attic insulation and will stand on the plaster or wallboard ceiling. To dry the insulation out, one must first pull the wet insulation away from the water area. If there is water standing on the plaster or wallboard ceiling, use a sponge or sponge mop and pail to pick up the standing water. If there is room in the attic to operate it, a wet/dry vac is best for water pickup and removal. Or make drain holes through the ceiling to let the water out (see Water Damage to Ceilings, p. 44).

The next step is to dry out the insulation. Because the insulation is contained in the attic, where there is little air movement, it will be difficult to dry. If there are windows or a power ventilator in the attic, open the windows or turn on the power vent to move a large volume of air through the attic. The moving air will pick up moisture from the insulation and will carry it outdoors. Forcing ventilation is the only way to quickly dry the insulation. If you don't have power attic vents, set one or more portable house fans in the attic. When you are sure all moisture has been removed, replace the insulation. A leaf rake can be a useful tool for removing and respreading blown Fiberglas insulation. **Note:** Wear a dust mask and goggles when working with Fiberglas.

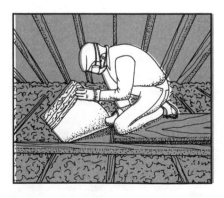

To dry water-damaged ceilings, pull back attic insulation. Use a sponge or wet/dry vac to remove water. Do not replace insulation until ceiling is dry.

ROOF SAFETY

Before deciding to do your own roof maintenance work, consider your own age and health limits. Climbing on ladders and roofs is definitely for the young and agile, so be sure you are physically up to the job.

If you feel fit to handle the physical demands of climbing, be sure you are dressed for the task. Over-the-ankle footwear can provide stability and insurance against ankle injury while climbing. For climbing or roof walking choose ankle-high boots with crepe rubber soles. The rubber soles provide slip resistance, while also protecting from damage the shingles you walk on. If clothing materials snag on a nail or rain gutter, the snag can cause you to fall. Wear snag-resistant pants, such as tough canvas blue jeans. Wear a long-sleeved shirt to protect yourself from abrasions and sunburn. A cowboy-style neckerchief can be tied to protect the back of the neck from sunburn, or can be tied over the mouth and nose to avoid breathing in dust or dirt. If you are doing extensive sanding or sawing, or spraying paint, choose an EPA-approved mask to protect yourself from breathing dust or paint particles. Wear a baseball-type hat to keep the sun and dirt out of your eyes and your hair. Don't climb with hands full of tools or materials. Instead, tie a clothesline rope to a 5-gallon plastic pail, place tools and materials in the pail, and pull the pail up to the roof via the rope. If you are shingling a roof, have the shingles delivered by a truck that is equipped with a conveyor belt to move the shingle bundles to the roof.

Check the weight limits of your ladder before climbing. Remember that the ladder must be able to carry both your weight and the weight of any materials or tools you will be using or carrying. Be aware that a metal ladder can be a shock hazard if the ladder contacts overhead electrical power lines. Be very careful to keep the ladder away from shock hazards as you move and work.

POWER TOOLS AND WATER

To protect the worker from shock, electrical power tools are double insulated or have a 3-prong grounded plug. These built-in tool safety features are sufficient, under most working conditions, to protect the worker from hazardous shocks. But the advent of battery-powered cordless tools has been a real plus for electrical safety when working around water or when in direct contact with a ground. If you haven't invested in a cordless drill yet, consider the safety advantage of cordless tools when you are working outdoors on concrete slabs or on wet ground. The advantages of cordless technology in protecting against electrical shock are even more important when you are working on or around boats or docks, metal fencing, or when installing equipment on or near grounded plumbing such as on private water wells or supply or drain pipes. A further safety advantage of cordless tools is just that: While climbing or working, there are no extension cords to trip over.

33 LEAKING PLUMBING

If you are living in your first house and do not understand the basic plumbing operation, take time to acquaint yourself with all the plumbing shutoffs. Though not a common occurence, you may need the information if you have a burst pipe or a leaking plumbing fixture such as a failed water heater.

To shut off all water flow throughout the house, look near the water meter where the water supply or street pipe enters the house. The water shutoff main valve, called a "gate valve," shuts off the main water supply to the house so there is no water pressure or flow at any fixture.

In addition to the main water valve, there are often shutoff valves at each plumbing fixture. These separate shutoff valves permit repair work to proceed on a fixture or faucet without having to shut off all water to the house, via the main valve. Look for shutoff valves under the sink in bathroom vanities, or under the kitchen sink, or on the incoming cold water pipe near the water heater, and beneath the water tank or closet behind the toilet bowl. Be sure every family member knows where the water shutoff valves are located, and that the valves can be turned off in a plumbing emergency.

Turn off water to the entire system at the gate valve, usually located on the main water supply pipe next to the water meter in the basement. Turn the valve clockwise; if there are two valves, turn off the valve on the supply side of the meter.

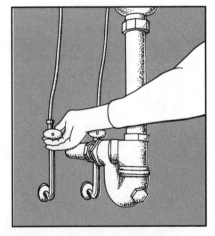

Turn off water to a fixture by locating the valve on the supply pipe under the fixture and turning it clockwise. A faucet will have two shutoffs: one for cold water and one for hot. If there are no shutoff valves, turn off the main water supply to the house.

BURST WATER PIPES

Steel piping in older houses may be subject to rust-through and bursting or leaking. Steel water pipes were assembled by threading the pipe, and cutting these threads reduced the wall thickness of the pipe, so rust-through and leaks usually occur near joints in the threaded portions of the pipes.

The good news is that leaks in plumbing pipes usually develop slowly, providing time for detection and correction. If there are steel water pipes in your house, check for any signs of leaking, paying special attention to the threaded portions of the pipes. If there is rust or signs of moisture at the joints, the steel pipes may be failing and the entire piping system may need replacement.

Epoxy pipe patches are available. These patches are made by blending together two strips of epoxy material. After blending the two epoxy strips, just wrap the doughlike epoxy material around the pipe leak. In most cases, however, you should consider the patch to be a temporary solution, because any rust-through of the pipe is usually a symptom of developing rust throughout the entire piping system. Then, the old piping must be removed and replaced by copper or plastic piping. Total pipe replacement is a job for a professional plumber.

35 FROZEN WATER PIPES

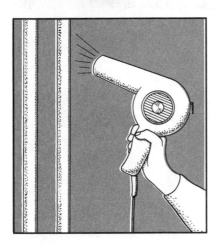

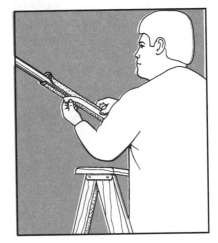

Use a hair dryer set to HIGH to warm a frozen pipe. Play the stream of hot air over a wide area to thaw evenly.

If pipes run through unheated areas like crawl spaces and garages, prevent them from freezing by wrapping them with pipe insulation. Slip the tubes over the pipe and use duct tape to seal the joints.

To prevent incoming water pipes from freezing, building codes have requirements that pipe ditches be dug so they are below the frost line, the depth to which the ground freezes. Ordinarily this prevents street-to-house supply pipes from freezing in winter. In unusually cold weather the frost may go deeper than normal, and water pipes may freeze. Moving water does not freeze so easily as standing water. If water pipes tend to freeze in winter and cold weather threatens, leave one faucet running slowly so water is moving through the pipes. If pipes do freeze, consider calling a plumber who has the expertise to thaw them safely.

Do not use a propane torch for thawing frozen pipes, because heat concentrated in one area can turn ice inside the pipe into steam and a dangerous explosion may result. For thawing water supply pipes use a heat gun or hair dryer. To avoid creating a steam explosion, do not apply heat to one small area of the pipe. Play the hot air from the gun or dryer over a wide area so that the pipe will thaw evenly.

If you have water pipes in an unheated area of the house (in a crawl space or attached garage), the best remedy is to insulate the pipes completely to prevent them from freezing. Electrical resistance heating cables can be wrapped around exposed water pipe and plugged into an electric supply. The heating cables should be used with care and only as a last resort. It is much better to insulate the pipes so they neither freeze nor require use of a heating cable.

36 WATER HEATERS

One way to avoid emergencies is to be aware of the life expectancy of your appliances. Both gas and electric water heaters have a life expectancy of 10 to 12 years, so if your heater is nearing the end of its expected lifespan it may be time to consider water heater replacement.

If you hear any strange noises coming from your water heater, such as rumbling, crackling, or hissing, turn the heater thermostat to "off." Then turn off the water supply valve on the cold water pipe above the water heater. Have the water heater inspected by a professional. If there is no hot water or you find a water puddle under the appliance, turn off the thermostat and water supply valve as above, and call a serviceman.

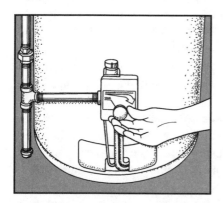

Turn the water heater thermostat to "off," then shut off the water supply valve.

37 PLUGGED SEWER DRAINS

The most common cause of plugged sewer drains is putting foreign objects into the sewer. The do-it-yourself (DIY) movement has contributed to this problem because DIYers sometimes put patching or repair materials into the drains. Common offenders include patch plaster, concrete, or wallboard compound that may remain in the sewer drain, harden, and cause plugs that are difficult to remove.

To avoid plugging sewer drain pipes, mix patching compound in a plastic pail. Allow leftover patching materials to harden in the pail, then flex the sides of the pail to loosen the patching compound. Place the hardened compound into the trash and dispose of it.

Don't use your sewer drains as a disposal. Never flush paper products other than toilet tissue down the drain. Put soap wrappers, facial tissues, and feminine-hygiene products into a wastebasket for disposal.

In the kitchen, dispose of grease and plastic or paper food wrapping in the wastebasket. When using the garbage disposer, let the water run long enough so that all food residue is flushed completely out of the small sink drains and into the larger main drains.

Don't wait until you have a plug to have your main drain cleaned. Instead, have a professional clean the main drain (between the house and the street main) periodically. This service will ensure that drain pipes remain open. Rather than having a flooded basement, and midnight drain emergency cleaning, the problem is transformed to a mess-free regular maintenance project. In most cities, depending on the length of the drain, professional main drain cleaning may cost between $50 and $100.

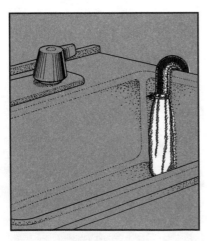

One way to minimize drain debris is to install a filter, made of stocking material, on the end of your washer's drain hose.

38 WATER WELL FAILURE

If you live in a rural or recreational area, the house water supply may be from a private well. If your well stops working, you can restore emergency water service from any house well nearby. You'll need enough garden hose to reach between the neighbor's outside faucet (also called a "bib faucet" or "sillcock") and your own. You will also need a hose connector, called a "male-to-male" connector, to hook the threaded male end of the hose to the threaded exterior faucet of your house. You can buy a male-to-male connector at hardware or plumbing supply stores.

To use a neighbor's well, attach the garden hose to the outside faucet on the neighbor's house. Then attach the other end of the hose, via the male-to-male connector, to your own outside faucet. Open both faucets and the neighbor's well will supply your house with water until repairs can be made. Don't neglect to shut off the water valve at your well. If you forget to shut your well valve before opening your exterior sillcock, the neighbor's water will just run back into your well.

39 TOILET WAX RING

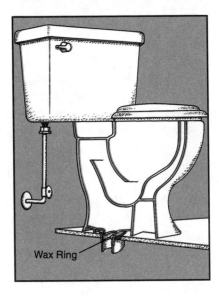

Wax Ring

A defective wax ring is quite often the culprit when water leaks from around the stool base of a toilet. As a stopgap measure, turn off water to the tank at the shutoff valve until the plumber arrives.

If you see water standing on a bathroom floor, check where the water is coming from. To find the leak source, it may be necessary to first mop up the water so you can follow the water stream. Water seeping from under the stool base, from between the stool and the floor, is an indication of a faulty wax ring. The wax ring is a doughnut-shaped device, made from plumber's wax, that is used to seal the joint between the toilet bowl or base and the toilet drainpipe. If the water appears to be seeping from under the toilet stool base, you can temporarily stop the leak by shutting off the water supply valve under the water tank. Then flush the toilet twice, to empty water both from the water tank and from the bowl. The leak will stop flowing when the bowl is empty.

The permanent repair is to replace the wax ring. This repair may be best left to a professional plumber, because to make the repair you must shut off the water, drain the water from the toilet system, remove the water tank from the toilet stool, and unscrew the retaining bolts that hold the stool atop the drain pipe. The last tasks are to install the new wax ring and reinstall the toilet bowl and tank.

If you decide to call a plumber to make the wax ring repair, you can use the toilet until the plumber arrives. Just turn off the water supply valve (located under the toilet tank) and flush the toilet. The first flush will empty the toilet tank. The second flush will empty the water from the toilet bowl so it cannot seep from under the wax ring. To use the toilet, you must turn on the water supply valve to fill the tank with water, flush to fill the toilet bowl, and then use the toilet. When you have finished, shut off the water supply valve and flush to empty the tank, then flush again to empty the bowl.

40 LEAD IN WATER

Recent studies have raised concerns about the dangers of lead poisoning from ingesting (either by drinking or cooking with) ordinary tap water. Reports emphasize that the greatest danger of lead poisoning by water comes from drinking water in houses where plumbers used lead solder to connect copper water supply pipes. Homeowners should fully understand the degree of the danger faced, and take steps to eliminate any lead danger to family members. Most lead solder was used in houses with soldered copper pipes, built before 1978. If you live in one of these houses, be aware that studies have shown that much of the lead may have leached out of the solder over the years. Also, realize that you cannot tell whether lead is present by looking at the water. Any lead in drinking water is dissolved and is not visible as particulate matter. The only way you can be sure whether water is lead-free is to have it tested. Hundreds of cities have recently conducted lead tests on their water supplies, so check with your own city water utility for a lead report before hiring an independent test firm.

If your tested water shows a high lead content, the culprit may be from lead solder used in older water faucets. To eliminate this lead source, replace your water faucets with new, lead-free models.

Dangers from lead exposure vary among people. Most at risk are infants who drink formula made with tap water that contains lead, then pregnant women, then young children. Experts suggest that you can make tap water safe for most people by allowing the water to run for a minute or two before drinking it. This lets the running water flush any lead residue out of the pipes.

For answers to other questions call the National Lead Information Center at 800-LEAD-FYI.

CHAPTER FOUR

125

HOME SECURITY, TESTS, AND ALARMS

TIPS

CARBON MONOXIDE TESTS

Carbon monoxide (CO) poisoning is a home health hazard that is especially common during the winter heating season. There are 230 *fatal* cases of carbon monoxide poisoning annually in the U.S., plus thousands more poisoning cases in which the victims are sickened but recover. Symptoms of carbon monoxide poisoning include flulike symptoms such as fatigue, drowsiness, weakness, shortness of breath, red or burning eyes, nausea, and persistent headaches.

What makes carbon monoxide so dangerous is that it is an odorless, tasteless, and colorless gas, so it is very difficult for a person to detect. It is produced by incomplete fuel combustion or poor ventilation of fuel-burning appliances such as oil or gas furnaces, gas cooking appliances, water heaters, fireplaces, or wood stoves. Another common source can be an auto engine left running in a attached, closed garage. Compounding the danger is the fact that as people act to tighten their houses with caulk and weather stripping, combustion appliances may not be able to draw in sufficient outside air for burning. This may cause a furnace to pull combustion gases back into the house, rather than exhausting them safely up the chimney.

In addition to being constantly alert for the physical symptoms mentioned above, any or all of which may signal a health-threatening problem, study the following checklist to avoid carbon monoxide poisoning:

- Have a professional check and adjust your furnace burner and controls to be sure the burner and vent systems are operating properly.
- Make frequent visual checks of the furnace. In the burner, look for yellow flames that indicate an improper gas and air combustion mix (blue flames indicate a proper gas and air mix), for excessive heat in the furnace area, and for rust and scaling in front of the furnace, below the vent. All these symptoms are warning signs of poor combustion or venting and should be checked out by a pro.
- Hold a lighted match or lighter under the draft hood on the gas water heater. If the match flickers downward or goes out, it may indicate dangerous exhaust backflow.
- Have a professional repairman check out any sudden appearance of moisture condensation on window panes or under windows. These symptoms may indicate ventilation or combustion problems in a forced-air furnace.

Film-badge sensor cards that turn color when carbon monoxide is detected may be purchased, but these badges provide protection only for a short period of time and monitor only the immediate area around the furnace. The Consumer Product Safety Commission (CPSA) and Underwriters Laboratory (UL) have recently announced their approval of carbon monoxide (CO) detectors for the home. These detectors look much like the familiar home fire or smoke alarms, are battery-operated, and emit a loud signal when they detect dangerous levels of CO. The alarms cost between $50 and $70 each and contain sensors that must be replaced every 3–5 years.

Look for carbon monoxide detectors at home centers. If they are not available off-the-shelf, ask the store manager to order one or more units for you. The approved units include CMD-1 and CMD-2, by BRK Electronics (First Alert brand); COS-200, made by Asahi Electronics of Canada; and CO-STAR Model 9B-1 by the Quantum Group in San Diego, California.

The film-badge sensor card has a pink/orange sensor that turns gray or black if carbon monoxide is present. Note the sensor is attached to the furnace cold air return and near the gas-fired water heater.

42 SMOKE ALARMS

According to fire expert Olin L. Greene, the U.S. has one of the highest fire death rates in the world. Each year in the U.S. 30,000 people are injured and 5,500 people (including 100 firefighters) die in fires. To put those figures in perspective, fires kill more people than tornadoes, floods, hurricanes, and earthquakes combined. In residential fires, more people die each year from smoke inhalation than from being burned. In today's homes, plastic materials such as carpeting and upholstery emit toxic fumes when they burn, making modern-day fires doubly dangerous. Smoke alarms can alert family members and can also provide valuable extra minutes in which to move the family to safety.

Smoke alarms may be battery-powered or hard-wired (connected to your house wiring). There are arguments for and against both types of alarm. Some experts warn that people often neglect to replace dead batteries, making battery-powered alarms potentially worthless. Those who favor battery-powered alarms point out that hard-wired alarms will fail to function if electrical wiring is damaged in the fire. The best advice may be to install at least one battery-powered alarm on each level of your house: in the basement

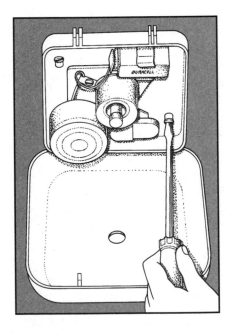

Smoke alarms are so easy to install that there's no reason for not having several in every home. You only need a screwdriver.

or other furnace or appliance area, where fires frequently originate; in a center hall, near bedrooms (most residential fires occur at night); and in or near the kitchen to warn of cooking fires. Other alarm locations to consider might be in attached garages and in laundry rooms or home workshops. Install smoke alarms on the ceiling or about one foot below the ceiling on the wall. The alarms are easy to install—most are held by two screws, supplied with the units—and you need only a screwdriver to make the installation. Most alarms have test buttons on their faces. Push the buttons once a month to be sure the units are operational and batteries are not dead. And make it a point to replace alarm batteries twice a year. To make it easy to remember, replace the batteries on the days when you reset home clocks in the spring for daylight saving time, and in the fall when you return to standard time.

43 RADON TESTS

Radon gas first became recognized as a health risk when it was detected in houses built with materials that had been contaminated by uranium mine wastes. Second only to smoking tobacco, radon is suspected of causing as many as 100 lung cancer deaths per day. A radioactive gas that is odorless, colorless and tasteless, radon is difficult to detect. You must use one or more test devices to determine whether you have a radon hazard in your house.

Radon is measured in picocuries, a unit of measure of radioactivity. A picocurie is one trillionth of a curie. The permissible limit for radon exposure in the home is set at 4 picocuries per liter of air, or 4pCi/l. To determine the level of personal risk, consider that your lung cancer risk from exposure to 4pCi/l of radon is statistically equal to the risk of dying in a home accident; the cancer risk at 20pCi/l radon exposure is equal to the individual's risk of dying in an auto accident.

To test for radon, buy a radon test cannister containing activated charcoal at a home center or department store. The charcoal acts as a filter to separate and trap radon particles. Open the cannister and leave it for 3 to 7 days in your basement or crawl space (or house, if there is no crawl space or basement and the house is built on a concrete slab). When the test period is ended, close and seal the cannister and send it off to the testing laboratory. The cost for the test, including postage and laboratory work, is usually about $25.

Another radon test device is called the alpha track unit. The test uses a sheet of polycarbonate plastic as a recording surface. The exposed plastic sheet is left in place for 3 to 6 months and is struck by alpha particles from the decaying radon. When evaluating the test, a laboratory technician counts the number of dents in the plastic to find the level of radon present. This test may cost between $25 and $50.

If these low-cost tests show no radon or radon levels under 4pCi/l, your home is safe, but be aware that radon levels may fluctuate, so it may be wise to retest periodically. If the tests reveal radon levels greater than 4pCi/l, do not panic. Radon levels can often be reduced by inexpensive steps such as caulking up cracks in basement floors or walls, by sealing concrete walls with waterproofing sealer such as UGL Drylok, or by increasing ventilation in the affected area. Check with your local building inspector or regional Environmental Protection Agency office for the name of an approved radon abatement contractor. Get several bids and check out abatement contractors carefully before signing any contract.

STATE—EPA REGION

Alabama—4	Kentucky—4	North Dakota—8
Alaska—10	Louisiana—6	Ohio—5
Arizona—9	Maine—1	Oklahoma—6
Arkansas—6	Maryland—3	Oregon—10
California—9	Massachusetts—1	Pennsylvania—3
Colorado—8	Michigan—5	Rhode Island—1
Connecticut—1	Minnesota—5	South Carolina—4
Delaware—3	Mississippi—4	South Dakota—8
District of Columbia—3	Missouri—7	Tennessee—4
Florida—4	Montana—8	Texas—6
Georgia—4	Nebraska—7	Utah—8
Hawaii—9	Nevada—9	Vermont—1
Idaho—10	New Hampshire—1	Virginia—3
Illinois—5	New Jersey—2	Washington—10
Indiana—5	New Mexico—6	West Virginia—3
Iowa—7	New York—2	Wisconsin—5
Kansas—7	North Carolina—4	Wyoming—8

EPA REGIONAL OFFICES

EPA Region 1
Room 2203
JFK Federal Building
Boston, MA 02203
(617) 223–4845

EPA Region 2
26 Federal Plaza
New York, NY 10278
(212) 264–2515

EPA Region 3
841 Chestnut Street
Philadelphia, PA 19107
(215) 597–8320

EPA Region 4
345 Courtland Street, NE
Atlanta, GA 30365
(404) 881–3776

EPA Region 5
230 South Dearborn Street
Chicago, IL 60604
(312) 353–2205

EPA Region 6
1445 Ross Avenue
Dallas, TX 75202–2733
(214) 655–7208

EPA Region 7
726 Minnesota Avenue
Kansas City, KS 66101
(913) 236–2803

EPA Region 8
Suite 1300
One Denver Place
999 18th Street
Denver, CO 80202
(303) 283–1710

EPA Region 9
215 Fremont Street
San Francisco, CA 94105
(415) 974–8076

EPA Region 10
1200 Sixth Avenue
Seattle, WA 98101
(206) 442–7660

If you have radon-related questions contact the regional office of the Environmental Protection Agency (EPA) for your state.

44 DETECTING NATURAL GAS

Leaking gas can be hazardous or fatal if it is inhaled, deadly if it causes an explosion. If you have a gas furnace or other appliance, be aware of the danger signals of a gas leak. Natural gas and propane are odorless and colorless. For safety reasons, gas distributors add chemicals that give the gas its common detectable odor. If you smell gas and suspect a leak, observe the following checklist:

- Check all gas appliances and find out where the gas turnoff valves are located. For reasons of safety and for servicing gas-fired appliances, there are lever-type shutoff valves in the gas lines near your furnace and range. You'll need to know where the gas valves are in case of emergency.
- Don't use a match or other open flame to check for gas leaks. Check the source of the gas odor. Often, it may be a leaking pilot light or gas burner. Turn off the gas to the appliance, and let the gas dissipate before trying to relight or repair the appliance.
- If the gas odor persists, get the family out of the house. Leave windows and doors open to help dissipate the gas. To avoid any dangerous sparks (which could ignite the gas), do not touch light switches or telephones. Go to a neighbor's house to call the gas company service department.
- If you detect any gas smell outdoors, it may mean a leaking gas pipeline. Leave the area and call the gas company.
- Before doing any digging on your property (excavations for room additions, for example), call your local gas company and ask the exact location of the gas lines. With this information you can avoid accidentally hitting and bursting a gas pipeline while digging.
- Keep the gas utility company phone number in your "emergency number" file so you can find it quickly in an emergency.

ASBESTOS

The media has so exaggerated the threat of asbestos that it has made do-it-yourselfers wary of removing the substance from a 9' × 12' linoleum floor. Actually, asbestos came to the attention of the public health authorities when, after years of exposure, career asbestos workers began to develop lung cancer and other respiratory health problems. Most of those afflicted worked for companies that made products containing asbestos, such as insulation, floor tiles, floor covering, wallboard taping compounds, pipe insulation, and brake shoes for cars. The asbestosis and other diseases the workers experienced developed only after long years of daily or regular exposure to asbestos. Most people will never contact enough asbestos fibers to cause health worries, because asbestos is now banned from use in most consumer products.

The potential asbestos danger is from breathing airborne asbestos particles. In most cases asbestos is in a static condition, not airborne, so there is no cause for worry. Even though your house may contain large amounts of asbestos covering boilers or hot water heating pipes, experts assure us that asbestos that is not damaged is not a hazard. The Environmental Protection Agency (EPA), in the booklet *Report to Congress on Indoor Air Quality*, reports a study comparing airborne outdoor asbestos levels with prevailing indoor levels in forty-three federal buildings that contained asbestos materials. The EPA report states: "An interim report . . . indicates no statistical difference between indoor and outdoor levels (of asbestos), even in buildings with damaged asbestos-containing materials."

Wear a dust mask when removing minor quantities of building materials that may contain asbestos fibers, such as ceiling tiles. If you are doing a major remodeling project that will disturb large amounts of asbestos, hire a pro to remove and dispose of the asbestos materials. Check with your local building department or the local office of the EPA for the name of a certified asbestos abatement contractor.

46 ELECTROMAGNETIC FORCE

Environmental concerns now include the possibility that electromagnetic forces (EMF) may pose a health risk. The sources of these electromagnetic forces include emissions from high-power electrical transmission lines that pass near your house, and various electrical devices, including electric blankets. While not at this time hoisting a red flag on the subject, the Environmental Protection Agency advises that we practice "prudent avoidance" of long-term exposure to more than 5 milliGauss of electromagnetism.

If you have high-power electrical transmission lines near your house, or suspect possible exposure from home electrical devices, you can buy an EMF detector for about $175. The detector is the size of a pocket calculator and measures magnetic fields from 1 to 1,999 milliGauss. The company that manufactures the EMF detector is Walker Scientific. Ask for the ELF-40D Field Monitor. Or, check the Yellow Pages under "Inspection Service" to find a home inspector who can perform the testing for you.

SECURITY ALARMS

According to national crime statistics, 25 percent of all houses (one out of four) will be burglarized this year. You can pay upwards of $3,000 to buy a professionally installed home burglary alarm system, but the budget-conscious do-it-yourselfer can install his own alarm system for a cost of $200 or even less. The total cost of your alarm system will depend on the type of system you choose, plus the number of options or sensors included.

Options include the hard-wired Safe House system from Radio Shack. The term *hard-wired* means the alarm is installed and connected directly to a house electrical power circuit, as opposed to being plugged in or battery-powered. The Safe House can incorporate a combination of magnetic switches, motion detectors, smoke detectors, and most other types of sensors.

Another type of do-it-yourself (DIY) alarm is the wireless system. The wireless system relies on radio waves rather than wire communications between the sensors and the control panel. These systems can be installed using only a screwdriver. If a wireless system has the capability to monitor its sensors to ensure that they are performing properly and are communicating with the control panel, it is called a "supervised" wireless. Supervised wireless systems employ computer technology to achieve the self-monitoring features. One inexpensive supervised wireless alarm is the Heath Zenith Model SS-6100. Some of these DIY systems can be connected to a full-time monitoring station.

Easiest to install and to work with are the self-contained systems. Like small appliances, self-contained systems can be plugged into a nearby outlet and moved as needed. One inexpensive self-contained system is the Vantage Technology Homewatch 2000, a $150 unit that can be hooked to hard-wired options and/or be connected to a full-time monitoring station.

48 MOTION DETECTORS

One effective and inexpensive security product is the motion detector light. These lights are available at home centers at a cost of $25 or less, including the floodlight bulbs. The motion detector uses infrared light to sense the presence of passing people or cars, and turns on the lights to either welcome friends or to warn trespassers. A typical model can sense movement within an arc that is 60 feet long and 60 feet wide.

The motion detector has three adjustments. One, marked "SENS," is a sensitivity monitor that determines the amount of heat needed to activate the sensor and turn on the light. Some are so sensitive that they can be

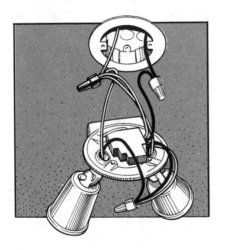

Turn off electric power to light. Remove the old fixture and install the motion sensor fixture. Use wire nuts to attach the fixture wires: black or red wires to the black (power) wire from the outlet box, white wire to white (neutral) wire in the outlet box, and green to green (ground) wire in the outlet box.

Carefully fold all wires behind the motion detector and use screws to secure the new fixture to the outlet box. Turn on power and test the light.

activated by the intrusion of a small dog or cat. The second adjustment is a built-in adjustable photo cell that permits the lights to be activated at a certain level of darkness ("DAYLIGHT"). This prevents activation of the light during daylight. The third ("TIME") control determines the length of time the light will stay on when triggered. One model, for example, is adjustable from a time minimum of 15 seconds up to 18 minutes.

To install a motion detector unit, first turn off the electrical power at the main fuse or service entry box. Remove the old light fixture and follow the instructions provided with the detector to install it. Remember that wires are color-coded: Fasten black or red fixture wires to the black (power) wire in the box; fasten the white fixture wire to the white (neutral) box wire, and the green (ground) fixture wire to the green wire in the box. Use twist-on wire connectors (wire nuts) to connect the fixture wires to the power wires in the outlet box. Tug on the wires to be sure they are secured together via the wire nuts. Then turn the power back on at the service box and test the light to be sure it is working properly. Turn the power back off, then fold the electrical wires into the outlet box. Use the new screws to fasten the motion detector to the outlet box, then turn the power on. You'll find that your new silent sentinel will provide you with a new sense of security from intruders, and that you will never have to approach the house in total darkness when you return from your own nocturnal jaunts.

HOME HAZARDS

According to the Consumer Product Safety Commission (CPSC), the most common causes of home accidents are stairs, glass doors, cutlery, glass bottles and jars, and home power tools.

To accident-proof your home:

- Be sure stairs are well lighted, treads are secure and nonslip or covered with low-pile carpet, and handrails are in place and securely fastened to the walls. Do not "store" brooms, sweepers, old newspapers, toys, or other objects on the stairs.
- Have a glazier replace the glass in patio and storm doors with unbreakable glass or plastic.
- Keep kitchen cutlery sharp. Most cutting accidents occur when workers try to force dull knives to cut. Keep cutlery in a wall-mounted holder, out of children's reach.
- Buy food and bath products only in plastic jars or bottles. Don't buy glass containers. If you are environmentally conscious, be aware that plastic containers are rapidly becoming easier to recycle than are glass containers.
- Keep stationary power tools locked away behind shop doors. Disconnect the cords on power shop tools. Use manufacturer's tool locks that are provided with tools. Buy cordless tools to avoid electrical shock, and to avoid a tripping hazard from using electrical extension cords.

50 CALLING 911

The national 911 emergency number is just that: an emergency number, to be called only when the police, fire department, or paramedics are needed *immediately*. If you're not sure whether the problem qualifies as an emergency, then err on the side of caution, and call 911 anyway. If the problem is not an emergency, dial "0" for operator or call your local police, fire, or health emergency number.

The first step is to find out what kind of emergency phone sevice is available in your community. The best is the "enhanced" 911 system. The term *enhanced* means that the 911 operator is immediately provided with telephone company data that tells him or her automatically where the phone is located, the telephone number from which the caller is calling, and the name of the person under which the telephone is listed, including unlisted phone numbers. These enhanced systems are superior because they save valuable time. The caller does not need to verbally report the location, phone number, or address of the emergency or emergency caller. If your 911 number is not enhanced, be sure to tell the operator the address and phone number immediately. This way, if the phone call is cut off, the operator has a record of where the call came from.

If you live in an area that does not have 911 emergency service, you can simply dial "0" for operator. However, it is always desirable that you memorize the phone numbers of local emergency services. Some emergency services and/or local phone companies may provide peel-and-stick listings of emergency numbers that can be attached directly to your telephone.

When calling 911, try to be calm. Take a deep breath and relax. Then provide:

- Location of the emergency (if not enhanced 911).
- Kind of emergency (fire, police, or medical).
- What is needed (police, ambulance, fire equipment).
- Information as to whether weapons are involved in the emergency.
- Number of persons involved.
- Obstacles or conditions that might interfere with help (e.g., a sick person locked in a house with a vicious dog).

Keep the information factual. Do not exaggerate, but try to relate the true degree of emergency. Do exactly what the 911 operator tells you. Never hang up unless you are instructed to do so.

CHAPTER FIVE

125

FIRE PREVENTION

TIPS

51 FIRE FACTS

We should take the time to become more aware of the terrible toll that house fires take on our nation each year. U.S. fire deaths per million people average about twice the average for other industrialized nations. Fire kills more people each year than floods, hurricanes, tornadoes, and earthquakes combined. Fire costs this nation an estimated $50 billion annually. Information from the National Fire Protection Association (NFPA) tells us that most of these losses are the result of human carelessness.

Consider these facts: In a recent year (1991), 4,670 people died in house fires. Of these, 1,270 (about 27 percent) were caused by smoking. Heating equipment failures caused 720 fire deaths (about 15 percent), while 680 deaths (15 percent) were deliberate, caused by arson or other incendiary acts. Electrical distribution problems accounted for 460 (about 10 percent) of all fire deaths, and another 440 (about 10 percent) were caused by children playing with fire. About 8 percent, or 360 deaths, were caused by carelessness while cooking, and 740 deaths, or about 16 percent, were due to all other causes combined.

The good news is that six out of seven houses in this nation have at least one smoke detector. The bad news is that fully one third of those detectors do not work. Reasons for the nonworking detectors range from failure to test periodically, to neglecting to replace dead batteries, to family members borrowing the detector batteries for use in other electrical gadgets such as bath scales or TV remote controls. Test detectors every week (on most detectors you simply push a button to test), replace batteries at least once a year or as needed, and never remove detector batteries for other uses. To easily remember battery replacement, replace the batteries on your birthday, on a holiday, or when you change the clocks for daylight saving time.

52 WHERE FIRES OCCUR

Fire is the third leading cause of accidental deaths in homes. To reduce this statistic, we must know where fire hazards are most likely to occur. In the home, 27 percent of fires start in the kitchen, and these fires are most often the result of human error, not faulty cooking appliances. About 22 percent of fires occur in the bedroom, living room, or den, and most of these are the result of careless smoking. Chimney fires account for about 8 percent of fires, and the laundry and heating areas each are the site of about 3 percent of house fires. Garages, bathrooms, closets, and halls each generate less than 3 percent of house fires.

Geographically, the southeastern U.S. has the highest fire death rate per capita, and these are mostly due to use of heaters in the home. Wood stoves are a major cause of fires in the northern U.S.

Those living in an urban or rural area are at much greater risk of dying in a fire than those living in suburban or small town settings. Around 800 fire deaths per year occur in apartments. Apartment fires annually account for about 20 percent, or 60,000, of all structural fires. About 80 people die in hotel or motel fires each year, and most of these deaths are victims of fires caused by smoking.

53 HOME FIRE SPRINKLERS

Most of us are familiar with commercial fire sprinkler systems, but we may be unaware that home fire sprinkler systems are also available. The sprinkler systems consist of a network of water pipes and an assortment of valves. Automatic sprinkler heads are installed at strategic locations in the water pipes and are mounted on room ceilings. When heat levels rise above usual room temperatures, the sprinkler heads are activated and sprinkle water into the rooms. These sprinkler systems can be connected to any home water supply and can be installed in a new home for a cost of about $1.50 per square foot of construction. The sprinklers also can be installed as a retrofit to protect existing housing. Fire officials estimate that fire deaths could be reduced by up to 90 percent if houses had sprinkler systems in conjunction with smoke alarms.

Advantages of home sprinkler systems include early fire control and personal protection. Home sprinkler systems are especially desirable for families with children, senior citizens, or handicapped members who have special fire protection needs.

An average of one hundred fire fighters die each year while fighting fires, and many more are injured. With fire sprinkler systems in homes, fires would be much less intense, and we could reduce the toll for fire fighters. The sprinklers also could reduce the tax load for fire service by reducing the number of fires.

Ask your local fire department for more information on home sprinkler systems, or write to: Residential Sprinkler Program, U.S. Fire Administration, NETC, Emmitsburg, MD 21727.

54 FIRE DETERRENTS

The first line of fire defense is to equip your house with one or more smoke detectors. An estimated 86 percent of U.S. homes have smoke detectors, but as many as 30 percent of these detectors may not be working, most often because of dead batteries. Test detectors and replace batteries annually, or when needed. Having smoke detectors can double your family's chance of surviving a fire. And remember, a whopping 64 percent of residential fire deaths occur in the 14 percent of homes that have no smoke detectors.

When shopping, be sure any bedding or upholstered furniture you buy is fire- or smolder-resistant. Check also to be sure that night clothing, such as children's pajamas, is flame-resistant.

Have furnaces, fireplaces, and heating stoves checked each fall to be sure they are working properly. Have a professional chimney sweep clean your fireplace or wood stove chimney to remove creosote and soot. Keep portable space heaters clean and properly adjusted; use only approved fuels—e.g., use only kerosene in kerosene heaters. Keep portable heaters away from combustible materials such as furniture or draperies.

To eliminate the most common fire source, quit smoking. Failing that, use large and deep ashtrays to catch ashes and butts; be sure to stamp cigarettes butts completely out; and keep matches and smoking materials away from young children. Residential fire sprinklers are now available that can be connected to home plumbing systems. These sprinklers can be activated at the fire source to localize and minimize injuries and property damage.

55 WHO IS MOST VULNERABLE TO FIRE?

The most likely fire victims are senior citizens, who die at more than twice the average rate. Children under five years of age also die at twice the national average rate, and 25 percent of these child fire deaths are the result of children playing with fire or matches.

Men are twice as likely as women to be injured or die by fire; African Americans die in fires at double the national average and Native Americans have the highest fire death rate of all ethnic groups.

56 FIGHT OR FLEE?

Time was when the advice to homeowners was to try to extinguish a house fire. It is still true that if you have the proper fire extinguisher handy, you may be able to stop a small fire before it can spread and destroy your entire house. But fire fighters today give this advice: When in doubt, don't fight. Run. The most important thing is to get all family members to safety. Property can be replaced. Why the change in strategy? There are several reasons why you should flee from a fire. First, in today's urbanized world professional fire fighters may be only minutes away. Thus you have professional people nearby who not only know how to contain fires, but also have the equipment needed to do the job.

There is another compelling reason why you should seek professional help rather than trying to battle a house fire yourself. Fire fighters point out that unlike the houses of yesterday many building components and furnishings in today's houses are made of plastics or other modern materials. When burned, these chemicals give off toxic fumes, so that if you breathe them in it may be your last breath. Examples of materials that may give off toxic fumes when burned include carpets and floor coverings, upholstery fabrics, insulation, and furniture. Fire fighters, of course, have masks that permit them to enter the fire area without fear of toxic exposures. Because of this special equipment and training, fire fighters advise that you let them handle the fire.

PATHWAYS TO SAFETY

As mentioned in Chapter Four, every house should have at least one smoke alarm on each floor or level, including the basement. Also, install an alarm in the hall outside each sleeping room. If you sleep with bedroom doors closed, also install an alarm inside the bedroom. Have the family listen while you check the alarm to be sure they can hear it and can recognize its sound when it goes off in an emergency. These alarms can provide precious extra minutes to allow family members to find their way to safety. The majority of fatal house fires occur at night, when residents are sleeping, and 80 percent of fire deaths occur in the sleeping areas. It can be very confusing to awaken from a sound sleep to find the house in flames, or to find that smoke has reduced the visibility to zero. That is why it is important to involve all family members in practice escape drills, so the well-rehearsed procedure becomes second nature. Don't wait until an emergency occurs to plan and practice emergency procedures.

Each family member should know that smoke and heat both rise. To stay below the smoke and heat, get out of bed and drop to the floor when the smoke alarm sounds. If the door is closed, lay the palm of the hand on the door to check the temperature. If the door temperature feels normal to the touch, open it part way and check to be sure the hallway is clear of fire. If no fire is visible, crawl down the hall to the stairway. Be careful as you approach any stairway, because the stair shaft can act as a chimney, drafting the fire upwards. If the stairway is free of fire, crawl down the stairs and out through the nearest door. If clothes catch fire, do not run. Running can cause the clothes to burn more rapidly. Instead, you should stop, drop, and roll: stop, drop to the floor or ground, and roll over as many times as needed to help put out the fire.

If a door feels hot to the touch, do not open it. Instead, turn to an alternate escape route, usually through a window. Make sure that there are two or more escape routes from every room in the house. If bedrooms are on the second floor, install escape ladders at windows to help occupants get to ground level. Teach family members to make an exit, pick up a chair or other object, and break out the glass if a window can't be opened.

It is a fire code violation to have sleeping areas in a basement, attic, or other area where there are no windows large enough to permit a secondary exit. If windows are too small for an adult to crawl through, replace them with larger windows. Be sure that there are at least two escape routes from any room where people sleep.

Many fire injuries result when one family member reenters a burning house to search for other members. When planning your family fire drill, agree on a meeting place, and practice the house evacuation several times so that every member understands the plan. Once outside, every family member should move quickly to a designated meeting place for a "roll call," so that you can be sure that everyone is outside and safe.

Make sure every family member knows the phone number of the fire department. Emphasize that the rule is escape first, then call the fire department from a neighbor's phone.

58 FIREPLACES

Few things are more satisfying than a fireside in cold weather, but a chimney fire in a fireplace can be an awesome and threatening event. Because you are dealing with an open flame, a fireplace can present a constant fire hazard. Proper fireplace management can keep the fire inside the firebox and thus ensure a friendly fire.

Don't burn trash or treated or painted lumber in your fireplace. These may give off toxic fumes. Burning wet or improperly seasoned wood, or letting a fire burn at a low rate, may produce a tarlike substance called creosote in the fireplace chimney. In time creosote can build up a thick coating in the fireplace chimney. Creosote is highly flammable, and the creosote buildup in the chimney itself may catch fire. The intense heat produced by a chimney fire may crack the chimney liners or flues, making the chimney unsafe.

Most experts agree that by burning only dry, well-seasoned wood you can reduce the amount of creosote produced by your fireplace. To season fresh-cut wood, split it and stack it loosely so air can circulate between the wood chunks. Split wood should season for a year before being burned. And leave the draft open enough so that any fire will burn briskly enough to be relatively smoke-free, because this more efficient combustion will produce less creosote. A fire screen or glass fireplace doors can prevent sparks or burning logs from popping out of the fireplace and setting a hostile fire. Always keep the fire screen or fire doors closed when there is a fire in the pit. Again, showing your children what happens when logs are burned will teach them how fire consumes whatever it touches.

At least once each year, before the heating season begins, have the fireplace chimney checked by a professional. Don't try to clean your own chimney. Have the job done properly, by a professional, at required intervals. The proper cleaning interval depends on how cleanly the wood burns, and how often you use the fireplace. Follow the advice of your professional chimney sweep and establish a proper cleaning schedule.

 **59   HEAT/FLAMES**

The fire danger from using tools that have open flames, such as propane or welding torches, is obvious. When soldering or when burning paint, be careful not to ignite nearby combustible materials such as wood framing or building paper. When burning paint off exterior siding, keep a garden hose and nozzle handy to use in case of fire. When you have finished burning paint off an area, wet it down with the hose to prevent fire from starting.

In recent years heat guns have become a popular alternative to using open flame or burners where heat is needed. Although heat gun manufacturers have pronounced them safe from combustion, there have been incidents where the heat guns were responsible for house fires. In one such incident a heat gun was blamed for starting a fire when used to burn paint off the soffit or overhang area of a house. In another case a heat gun was blamed for igniting the kraft vapor barrier on batt insulation concealed in a wall. To test your own heat gun, turn it on high heat and hold it a few inches away from a scrap of paper. You may find that the gun indeed can start a fire, so you should use extreme care when using the heat gun around any combustible materials.

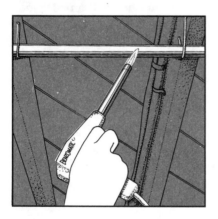

When using an open flame such as a propane torch for do-it-yourself chores, be very careful to avoid igniting combustible materials, and keep a hose or fire extinguisher handy.

60 WORKSHOPS

To minimize fire danger, keep shops and work areas clean. To limit exposure, buy chemical products in small quantities, and safely dispose of unneeded leftover home and shop chemicals. Keep work areas clean and free from wood scraps and sawdust. Dejunk work and storage areas, and dispose of trash, waste paper, and scrap building materials. Don't store trash near a furnace or heater where it might start a fire.

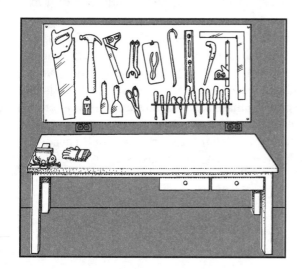

61 COMBUSTIBLE MATERIALS

Read and observe all container label warnings for combustible chemicals. Remember that the fumes of flammable chemicals are also flammable, and that it is dangerous to breathe the fumes if the label warns that the chemical is "harmful or fatal if swallowed." Also, the warning to use "with adequate ventilation" in fact means to use the chemical only when outdoors, or when ventilation is equal to being outdoors. Ventilation is not adequate if you can smell the fumes from the product. Augment available ventilation with exhaust or window fans.

Chemicals that pose a danger of fire or explosion are so marked. In order of flammability, the listings are combustible, flammable, and extremely flammable. Some paint solvents and strippers are designated as combustible or flammable, and these should never be used near open flames or appliance pilot lights. To avoid buying or using these solvents, buy latex or water-based paint products rather than alkyd (oil-based) products.

So that they can be identified, always store paint or combustible chemicals in their original containers, and be sure containers are equipped with tight-fitting lids.

62 HAZARDOUS WASTE DISPOSAL

Much has been written about the incorrect disposal of hazardous waste chemicals used in the home or yard. However, many local governments lack provisions for safe disposal of hazardous waste. Here are recommended disposal methods for most hazardous household wastes.

The following chemicals can be flushed down the toilet or sewer drain: auto antifreeze; cleaning products, including bleaches, window cleaners, ammonia products, and pine oil cleaners; liquid cosmetics; nonprescription and prescription drugs, except for chemotherapy drugs (ask pharmacist for instructions); nonchlorinated solvents (those that are not water soluble), including alcohol, acetone and methyl ethyl ketone. **Note:** If a cleaning product contains solvents or has label warnings such as "flammable" or "poison," check with local authorities for disposal instructions.

Pour these chemicals into an absorbent such as kitty litter and let the fumes evaporate before putting in the trash: chlorinated solvents (look on the label for "chloro-"); paint products such as mineral spirits, paint, or lacquer thinner; and liquid waxes and polishes. Spray leftover aerosol products into a cardboard box filled with absorbent material, and dispose of the aerosol container and the box in the trash.

Both latex and oil-based paints should be used up or given away to a church, charity, or theater. Small amounts can be left, with the can lid off, to dry up and then be thrown into the trash. To dispose of liquid pesticides, place absorbent such as kitty litter in a double plastic trash bag, pour in the pesticide, seal the plastic bags, and place in the trash. For powder pesticides wrap the containers in newspapers, place in a plastic trash bag, seal, and throw in trash. Dispose of used auto oil at service stations. **Note:** Above instructions apply in areas where no hazardous waste disposal facilities exist. Hazardous wastes such as oils, acids, fuels, pesticides, and oil-based paints and solvents should be recycled or taken to hazardous waste disposal sites *if available.*

CHECKLIST
HAZARDOUS WASTE DISPOSAL

PRODUCT	HOW TO DISPOSE OF IT
Aerosols	Use up product or spray remainder into a cardboard box, spray out propellant, dispose of container and box in trash
Antifreeze	Sewer drain
Cleaning products, liquid	Bleaches, window cleaners, ammonia products, pine oil cleaners: flush down toilet
Cleaning products, solid	Waxes, polishes: place in trash
Cosmetics, liquid	Flush down toilet
Cosmetics, powder	Dispose in trash
Drugs, nonprescription	Flush down toilet
Drugs, prescription	Dispose of leftovers in sewer drain; do not flush chemotherapy drugs into drain—ask pharmacist for instructions
Engine oil	Recycle at service station
Paint, latex	Let dry out in can and throw away or spread on newspapers and throw away
Paint, oil-base	Give to church, charity, or theater or let dry up in can and throw away
Pesticides, liquid	Place absorbent material in double plastic trash bag, pour in liquid pesticide, seal bags and place in trash
Pesticides, powder	Wrap container(s) in newspapers, place inside plastic trash bag, seal, dispose of in trash
Pressure-treated lumber	Dispose of scraps in trash. Don't burn: may give off toxic ash
Solvents, chlorinated (check label for "chloro-")	Pour into absorbent such as kitty litter, let evaporate, dispose of in trash
Solvents, nonchlorinated (not water-soluble)	Alcohol, acetone, methyl ethyl ketone: flush down sewer drain
Solvents, nonchlorinated (water-soluble)	Mineral spirits, paint or lacquer thinners: pour into absorbent material, let fumes evaporate, dispose of in trash

To dispose of hazardous household chemicals, the best solution is to use them for their intended purposes. Follow label directions for disposal of any leftover chemicals properly.

63 GASOLINE

To fuel garden and lawn equipment, most of us keep gasoline around the house. Although gasoline is a highly flammable and potentially explosive material, it is often carelessly handled by the consumer. While consumer warnings abound for such threats as radon or asbestos, gasoline is by a large margin the most dangerous substance found in most homes. Observe all safety warnings for handling gasoline.

- Buy gasoline in small quantities and store it in a laboratory-approved safety container in a shed or detached garage, never in the house.
- Do not use gasoline to start a fire in a fireplace, wood stove, or a charcoal grill.
- Do not use gasoline as a solvent for cleaning tools or machine parts, and never use gasoline indoors for any purpose.
- Do not use gasoline or any combustible chemical near a water heater, furnace, or other appliance pilot light. Remember that gasoline fumes are heavier than air and settle near the floor, where they may be ignited by a pilot light.
- Never leave gasoline within the reach of children. Explain to children that the containers are red as a danger warning, and to stay away from any red container.
- Let lawn equipment engines cool before refueling them. Gasoline spilled over a hot exhaust can be potentially deadly.

Use a fire safety can for refueling gas-fired home equipment. Do not refill lawn mowers or other equipment when the engine is hot.

TEACHING CHILDREN ABOUT FIRE

Friendly fire is the term used to describe any desirable or useful fire, such as the fire in the furnace burner that keeps us warm or the cookstove burner fire that cooks our meals. For most children, their first contacts with fire are with such friendly fires, and the child learns to think of fire as being friendly.

But just as the child learns that friendly fire is a blessing, he must also learn that uncontrolled or hostile fire can be dangerous. Experts suggest that simply telling the child that he shouldn't play with matches or fire may not make a lasting impression on the child. Rather than trying to impress the child by making this suggestion, crumple a sheet of newspaper in the fireplace or in a metal pail outdoors. Then, with the child looking on, light the sheet of newspaper and watch with the child as the paper is reduced to ashes. Then, explain to the child that any accidental fire can do the same thing to his home and belongings, and that is why he must never play with matches or fire. Watching the paper turn into ashes is a much more impressive example than a simple verbal plea.

65 FIRST AID FOR BURNS

If initiated quickly, the proper first aid can reduce the pain and severity of burns. If a person's clothes are on fire, the proper steps are to stop (moving will fan the fire), drop to the ground or floor, and roll over to smother the fire. When the flames are extinguished, move the victim from the area of danger. Call the emergency number, 911, immediately so that professional help can be sent. While waiting for paramedics to arrive, cool the burn area with cold water. If the burn is from chemicals, try to find a hose or hold the affected area under running water so you can continuously flush the burn area.

Never apply grease, butter, or ointment to a burn. The grease or oil may seal the heat in the flesh and aggravate the severity of the burn.

If skin is blistered, do not remove clothing that is stuck to the burned flesh. Pulling off such clothing may extend the damage to the skin.

To keep the burn area clean and free of dirt, cover the burn with a clean sheet or towel.

To reduce the severity of the burn, hold the burn area under cold water or place a cold wet towel over the affected area.

66 ARSON

In an average year six thousand Americans will die in fires. Some are trapped in rooms with no available fire exit; most of these die from smoke inhalation; many die from arson, or fires that are maliciously set. In addition to the cost in human life, the average arson fire costs $16,000. The insurance payoffs for arson not only help drive up the cost of fire fighting, in taxes paid, but also increase fire insurance costs for every American.

Fire marshalls nationally are pleading for public help in stopping arson fires. Here is a list of steps we all can take to reduce the number of arson fires.

- Don't leave gas or other flammable materials around where they might be used in an arson fire.
- Cut grass and weeds to reduce the ease of starting a fire on your property.
- Check your property frequently for burned materials, matches, or other signs of fire activity. The pile of ashes near your house foundation may mean that someone tried to set fire to it, and may return for another try.
- To prevent entry of intruders, lock storage areas such as garages or yard sheds.
- Keep an eye on neighborhood children, and report any sign of playing with fire to the parents or to authorities.
- Organize a neighborhood watch, and be on the lookout for suspicious strangers in the area.
- Be alert to any midnight moves in area businesses or homes. People secretly moving office equipment out of a business or expensive appliances out of a house may signal that an arson fire for insurance is planned.
- Take seriously any arson threats by irate neighbors or others. They may in fact be carried out.

If you see any of the above or other suspicious activity, report it to the police or to your local fire department. They will be happy to check it out. If, after a fire has already occurred, you recall having seen some suspicious prefire activity, call your local fire marshall and report it to him. For example, both fire fighters and police are increasingly reporting success in fighting crime because citizens with cellular phones are reporting crimes as they happen. With the help of these on-scene reports, authorities are able to act quickly and catch the perpetrators.

67 FALSE ALARMS

In an average year U.S. fire departments may respond to one million false alarms. That total includes both malicious and accidental activation of automatic fire alarms. In 1986 there were five false alarms for every four structure fires. Fire fighters must respond to every alarm, and in areas where false alarms are common extra fire personnel and equipment must be maintained to ensure that all alarms, both real and false, are answered. This extra burden of false alarms not only costs taxpayers and insurance companies huge amounts of money, but often costs fire fighters their lives. Racing to a fire is a dangerous business.

Children, unaware that a false alarm is a dangerous and costly crime, sometimes set off fire alarms as a prank. Children can be taught how serious a false alarm can be. In many areas fire fighters or a burn center representative will counsel children who set false alarms, and special class activities can redirect a child's antisocial behavior toward more constructive activities.

All citizens, including responsible children, should know where fire alarms are located in schools, churches, or other public places. Instruct children when and how to use a fire alarm. Remember that the person who sounds a fire alarm should stay by the alarm box to direct the fire fighters to the fire.

68 DIY HAZARDS AND CHILDREN

Do-it-yourself (DIY) home repair activity has increased rapidly over the past twenty years. As certain DIY activities increase, the danger of home fires or explosions also grows. Exercise caution when you are working with heat or fire, or with any flammable chemicals. Be especially wary when children are about and declare work areas "out-of-bounds." Store flammable DIY products well out of the reach of children.

69 FIRE EXTINGUISHERS

As noted earlier, in most cases fire fighters today recommend that you call the fire department rather than trying to fight a fire yourself. There are several reasons for this recommendation. First, you may waste valuable minutes vainly fighting the fire, minutes in which professionals could be en route to or fighting the fire. Also, the house and its contents may give off toxic smoke as they burn, and breathing those fumes can be deadly.

If you decide to fight the fire, be sure you have the proper type of fire extinguisher. Class A extinguishers can be used on ordinary combustible fires, such as wood, cloth, paper, or rubber. Class B extinguishers should be used on flammable liquids such as alkyd paints, oil, grease, gasoline, or flammable gas. Class C extinguishers should be used on fires involving energized electrical equipment, including wiring, fuse bases, circuit breakers, machinery, and appliances. Many homeowners choose an all-purpose ABC extinguisher for all-around use.

You must know how to use the extinguisher. The rules say to stand six to eight feet from the fire and observe the four-step PASS procedure. PASS stands for: Pull the pin to unlock the operating level; aim low, at the base of the fire; squeeze the lever below the handle to release the extinguishing agent; sweep from side to side and continue until the fire is out.

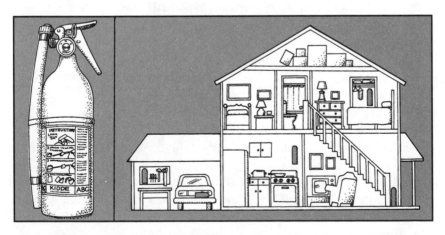

An ABC-rated home fire extinguisher may be the best all-around choice. The ABC designation means it can be used on any type of fire. Place a fire extinguisher in the garage, car, utility room, and kitchen. For maximum safety there should be an extinguisher on every floor of the house.

70 LIVING AREAS

Most fires are caused by carelessness. You can reduce your chances of having a fire by doing a little preplanning. Make a tour of your house and look for possible fire hazards. Here is a checklist to get you started.

- Be very careful with cigarettes. The ideal solution to cigarette fire dangers would be to quit smoking. If you must smoke, don't smoke in bed or when you are sleepy, and provide only large, deep ashtrays for smokers. Burning cigarettes may fall out of small or shallow ashtrays.
- Don't empty "hot" ashtrays—those that contain fresh butts—into wastebaskets, where they might start a trash fire. After an evening party, let ashtrays sit until morning.
- Before leaving home or going to bed, check under couch and chair cushions for smoldering butts.
- Don't leave matches or cigarette lighters lying about, especially if there are children in the house. Keep all fire and smoking materials in a high cabinet, preferably one with a locking door, where children cannot reach them.
- Keep portable heaters at least three feet away from drapes, furniture, or other combustibles. Turn portable heaters off if you leave the house or go to bed. Don't leave children alone in an area where a portable heater or wood stove is operating.
- Use only approved fuel in any heater: well-seasoned wood in wood-burning stoves or fireplaces, kerosene in portable kerosene heaters.
- Never leave cooking food unattended where a child might be tempted to sample hot or boiling items.
- To avoid grease fires, keep the stove and oven clean.
- Wear close-fitting clothes when cooking. Loose, hanging clothing can catch fire if allowed to drape over a flame.
- Place cooking pots on back burners and turn handles inward, over the cooktop, so children cannot reach them.
- Don't leave towels or pot holders on the cooktop where they might catch fire.
- Don't pour water on a grease fire. Burning grease can spatter and spread the fire. Instead, turn off the burner and slide a cover over the pan to smother the flames. Or keep an ABC-rated (all-purpose) fire extinguisher at hand.
- Don't hang combustibles over the cooktop. Don't hang curtains at a window near the cooktop.

98

71 CEILING LIGHT FIXTURES, BULBS

A burning incandescent light bulb can generate a lot of heat. An exposed bulb that is perpendicular to the ceiling can dissipate heat into surrounding air, but a bulb in a light fixture that sets flush against a ceiling lacks this protective air barrier, and can overheat and scorch or burn the ceiling. To prevent overheating and possible ignition of ceiling materials, flush-mounted ceiling light fixtures usually have insulation in their bases.

Inspect the label on all flush-mounted ceiling light fixtures. On most fixture labels there will be a warning to use only bulbs of limited wattage. Most such warnings limit bulb usage in the fixture to either 40 or 60 watts maximum. This warning is provided because using larger or higher-wattage bulbs can cause the fixture to overheat, possibly causing a fire. To avoid a fire, always strictly observe the bulb wattage limitations as listed on the fixture.

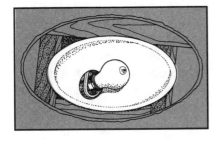

Ceiling light fixtures that provide little clearance around the bulb will easily overheat if improper high-wattage bulbs are used.

72 CHRISTMAS TREES

A Christmas tree fire is an all too common Christmas tragedy. The combination of a flammable tree and electric lights can be explosive, even deadly. One solution is to invest in an artificial Christmas tree, but many people still cling to using the traditional live tree. To ensure that you have none but merry Christmases, heed these tips from the National Christmas Tree Association.

- Check the tree for freshness. When shopping at the tree lot, grasp tree branches about six inches from the tip. Slide your hand toward the tip and check for falling needles. Needles commonly fall continuously on the interior tree branches, but the needles on the outer branches should be firm and should not fall easily.
- Pick the tree up and hold it about a foot above the ground. Now tap the stump of the tree on the ground and check for needle loss.
- Also check the fragrance and color of the tree. The fresh tree should be a deep green and should give off an "evergreen" fragrance.
- At home, stand the tree alone and let the limbs settle into place. Tree sap naturally seals the stump of a cut tree so the tree cannot take up water through the stump end. At the base of the tree make a fresh cut about ¼ inch above the old cut, so water can enter the tree fibers.
- Always use a watering-type tree stand. Buy a tree stand that will hold at least one gallon of water. Check the water level in the stand basin frequently. Trees may drink a lot of water when first placed in the stand.
- Check the needles frequently to see if they are drying out or if there is excessive needle loss.
- Position the tree away from heat sources such as a heater, fireplace, or TV set.
- Check tree lights to be sure wire insulation is intact and bulbs are tight. Unplug the tree lights when you go out or retire for the night.
- Dried evergreen trees burn with explosive force. To reduce fire exposure limit the time the tree is up. Plan to put the tree up no more than a week or two before Christmas, and take the tree down as soon as Christmas is over.

73 FIRE INSURANCE

Adding fire fighting equipment to the home is actually inexpensive insurance against fire loss or injury to your family. Still, you may be able to reduce your fire insurance premiums significantly if you add such equipment. To take advantage of the savings, you must notify your insurance agent of any additions you make. Premium savings vary among insurance companies, so you must contact your own agent to find out if you are eligible.

Adding smoke alarms, fire extinguishers, second-story fire ladders, or a home fire sprinkler system to your home can result in premium savings. Rewiring your house electrical system can earn an 18 percent reduction in insurance costs from one company. The rewiring must be done by a licensed electrician, and you must supply a certificate from your electrical inspector. Call your own insurance agent to find out what savings might be available for your particular project.

CHAPTER SIX

125

ELECTRICAL, HEATING, APPLIANCES

TIPS

74 CHECK THE LABELS

When buying electrical appliances, tools, or cords, be sure to read all label information and observe operator instructions in the owner's manuals. Look for an Underwriters Laboratories Inc. (UL) label on the product, which indicates that the product has been tested and approved for its intended use by the UL. The label will also list the watt or amperage consumption of the electrical device. But be aware that no amount of product testing can ensure the citizen against the dangers of careless operation. Only the operator can be responsible for the end use of the product.

After familiarizing yourself with the product, place all manuals, instructions, and warranty and repair information in a file envelope for future reference. If the tool or appliance needs service or repair, take it to an authorized service center.

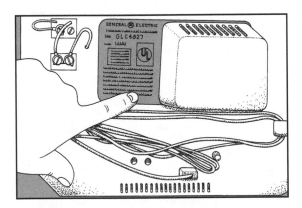

Read the label information and the owner's manual for all appliances. For easy future access, file all warranty and instruction information in an appliance file.

75 TELEPHONE SAFETY

Few appliances seem as safe and familiar to us all as the telephone, but remember that it can be a source of electrical shock or fire if it is used improperly. To avoid personal injury, follow these phone safety tips.

- Never use a telephone during an electrical storm. Lightning can strike telephone wires or equipment and can produce dangerous shocks.
- Never use a telephone that has been damaged in a storm or a fire. To find a repairman, consult your local telephone company or the manufacturer of your phone equipment.
- Never use a telephone in a shower or pool.
- Don't let children or pets chew on telephone cords or on the power cord of any electrical appliance.
- Don't use a phone if you smell gas. A spark from the phone may ignite the gas and cause a fire or explosion. If gas is present, go to a pay phone or a neighbor's phone to call the gas company for help.
- When changing or replacing a removable phone cord, always disconnect the cord from the jack first, then from the phone handset. When connecting a phone cord, connect the cord first to the phone, then to the phone jack.

76 ELECTRIC SERVICE ENTRY (MAIN) PANEL

Electricity enters your house via the service entry panel. Today's houses have three incoming electrical power wires: two hot or "live" wires and one neutral wire. In the entry panel box the live wires are usually black and red; the neutral wire is white or bare. A three-wire system lets you use both 115 volt and 230 volt circuits, so you can power appliances such as air conditioners and electric ranges. To create a 115-volt circuit, you combine the black or red and white or neutral wire; to create a 230-volt circuit you combine the red and black wires.

The three power wires are connected to the electric meter, then run to the fuse or circuit breaker panel. From the main panel the power wires branch into separate circuits and are routed throughout the house. Large appliances such as cooktops or ovens and electric clothes dryers may have their own circuits and fuses or circuit breakers.

Each circuit is protected by a fuse or a circuit breaker. These can be used to shut off power to the individual circuits. In case of an emergency, such as a fire or basement flood, or when you have to work inside the panels, there also is a main switch or circuit breaker to shut down the power to the entire house. The main power may be shut off via a lever, a circuit breaker, or a fused pull-out.

For your own safety, you should become familiar with the inside of the entry panel. Know what kind of main shut-off you have, and which fuses or circuit breakers control each of the circuits.

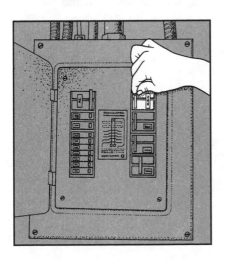

Before an emergency arises, study the electrical service entry panel so you know how to shut off power to the entire house. The main shutoff should be marked. It may be a lever, a fused pull-out, or a circuit breaker.

 **EXTENSION CORDS**

Here is a checklist of things to remember when buying or using extension cords.

- Never leave an extension cord plugged in when not in use. Children can play with live extension cords with disastrous results.
- Never use an extension cord that has been damaged or cut. Never try to repair a damaged extension cord. Replace it.
- Touch extension cords to be sure they are not hot. If a cord becomes hot, unplug it and do not plug it in again until an expert has checked the cause of the heat buildup.
- Some extension cords have a third or grounding plug, and others have one plug blade that is wider than the other (polarized cords). Never file or cut the plug of an extension cord to modify it to fit an odd outlet.
- Never run an extension cord under a rug or carpet, or over a heater, furnace, or anything that will raise its temperature.
- When working outdoors, use only extension cords that are rated for outdoor use.
- Never run extension cords through standing water or over any wet surface, such as a wet floor or grass.

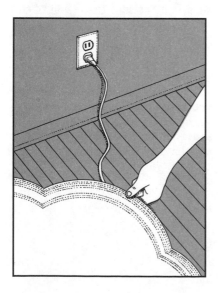

To prevent a fire, do not run an extension cord under a rug or over a furnace or other heating appliance. This may cause a heat buildup and possible fire.

78 PLUG ADAPTERS

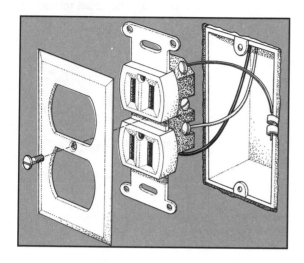

To ensure a good ground, adapters should be attached to the receptacle screw via the grounding ring or pigtail.

If your house, appliances, and power tools have all been purchased within the last decade or so, chances are that they all fit perfectly well together. But if the house and electrical contents are of varying vintage, you may have 2-slot electrical receptacles, and 3-prong plugs on your vacuum sweeper or power drill. Obviously, you cannot fit a 3-prong plug into a 2-slot receptacle. The ideal solution is to have an electrician bring your house wiring up to today's code requirements. If you have your electrical service updated and get a new certificate of code compliance from the contractor, you may be able to get up to 20 percent premium reduction from your fire insurance agent. You also will have a house that is much more efficient to live and work in.

The short-term solution may be to use an electrical plug adapter so you can use your 3-prong plugs in 2-slot receptacles. On the face or room side the plug adapter usually has two slots to receive the hot and neutral blades of the plug, plus a third hole for the grounding prong. On the wall or recep-tacle side there are two blades to fit in older 2-slot electrical receptacles.

That's as far as many people get when using the plug adapter. By just plugging the adapter into the receptacle and plugging the appliance into the adapter, you can use the device. But for safety, there is also a grounding ring or a pigtail wire on the plug adapter. To use the adapter properly, you should remove the screw holding the outlet cover plate to the existing receptacle, then secure the grounding ring or pigtail to the receptacle via the cover screw. This should ground the tool or appliance through the metal outlet box. Be aware, however, that these older systems were grounded by metal-to-metal contact of the circuit wiring components. To ensure a good ground, clean the old receptacle screw and contacts so they are free from plaster or paint.

79 GFCI RECEPTACLES

The fuse or circuit breaker at your electrical service entry panel is designed to shut off the current if a short or an appliance failure occurs on that electrical circuit. These safety devices can help prevent electrical fires. But the fuse or circuit breaker protection does not react quickly enough to protect people from dangerous or even fatal electrical shock, so modern electrical codes require Ground Fault Circuit Interrupter (GFCI) receptacles at outlets where shock hazards are greatest. GFCI receptacles are required where water or moisture is present to increase the shock danger. Bathroom, kitchen, laundry, garage, and exterior receptacles must have GFCI protection.

How does a GFCI work? In an electrical circuit the black or hot wire carries the current to the outlet or fixtures, and the same current returns to the service panel via the white or neutral wire. The GFCI device monitors the current flowing along both wires. As long as the current that is on the incoming black (hot) wire is equal to the current returning on the white (neutral) wire, there is no short or grounding of any current. However, if a person begins to experience a shock, some current goes to ground. The GFCI

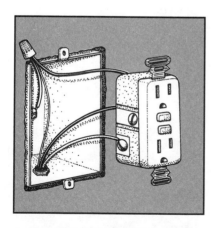

A GFCI that is designed to protect a single outlet is installed like any electrical receptacle. Other GFCIs may be installed in the entry panel, or in the receptacle nearest the entry panel, to protect all receptacles on that circuit.

then senses a drop in current of as little as 4 milliamps on the returning white wire and shuts off the current before the person is harmed.

In newer homes electrical circuits are protected by GFCI circuit breakers at the entry box. There are also two types of in-receptacle GFCIs. One type has two sets of black and white wires, and can be installed in the electrical outlet nearest the service panel to protect the entire circuit. Also available are GFCI receptacles that have a single pair of black and white wires and protect only the single outlet in which they are installed.

GFCI receptacles are inexpensive and are available at any home center or electrical supply store. They are sold complete with do-it-yourself instructions and diagrams. If your house has no GFCI protection, consider hiring an electrical contractor to update your electrical system by installing GFCIs at all outlets as mandated by current electrical codes.

80 SHOCK HAZARDS, TOOLS

Modern electrical hand tools feature better design, greater performance range, and greater worker safety than in the past. Today's tools not only have extra safety features, they also have plastic housings and double insulation features to reduce shock hazards. So, even though your old drill or saw may show no inclination to give up after a quarter century or more, consider turning in your older power tools for the greater utility and safety of modern tools.

A common hazard for electrical shock is using electrical power tools around water or wet locations. Be sure that any electrical tool you use in a damp or wet location is double-insulated, and is plugged into a GFCI-protected receptacle. Don't work at all in a situation where you will be standing or kneeling in the wet soil or grass, thus presenting a perfect ground path for any electrical short.

Where possible, use cordless battery-powered tools in wet locations. If you are working around a boat, boat dock, or swimming raft, avoid corded power tools. Also be wary of any contact with heating equipment or ducts or with plumbing pipes when you are using older corded power tools. Heating ducts and plumbing pipes present a near-perfect path for a short circuit to go to ground, and if you touch them while using a defective tool your body will complete the ground. If the tools needed for a wet project are not available in cordless style, then hire a professional to do the necessary work. The pros are equipped to work in all conditions, and can approach the job safely.

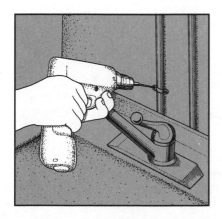

If possible, use a cordless tool when working around water, or on grounded components such as the plumbing and heating systems.

81 REPLACING A FIXTURE

When replacing a lighting fixture, first turn off electrical power at the service entry box. Remove the existing fixture, noting all wiring connections.

- Use the mounting hardware supplied with the fixture.
- Do not twist or tape fixture and electrical service wires together. Use only UL-approved electrical connectors, called wire nuts or Scotch Locks.
- Some wire nuts lock onto the wires and cannot be unscrewed. If you cannot remove the wire nut by turning it, pinch the end of the plastic nut with electrician's pliers to release the wire lock.
- Note that wire nuts or connectors are available in various sizes, the size depending on how many wires will be held together. Use the proper size wire nut.
- Remember that electrical wires are color-coded. Connect black wires (hot) to black wires, white wires (neutral) to white wires, and bare copper or green wires (grounding) to the bare or green grounding wires in the box.
- After connecting the wires together, pull each wire gently to test if it is firmly held by the wire nut. If any wire is loose, remove the wire nut, hold the wire ends together, and twist the wire nut on.
- Fold the wiring carefully and tuck it into the electrical box. Replace the fixture cover and turn on the power. Test the fixture to be sure it is working properly.

REPLACING A BULB

Replacing a bulb is a straightforward job, but certain precautions should be taken.

- Be sure hands are dry before working on electricity.
- Turn off the fixture switch and flip the circuit breaker or remove the fuse at the service entry (main) box.
- To prevent fixtures from overheating, maximum bulb size is usually indicated. Check the fixture label to find out how large a bulb can be used. Do not use an oversize bulb. If there is no listed bulb size, replace the old bulb with a new one of the same wattage.
- To screw in the bulb, hold it by the glass end only. To avoid electrical shock, never touch the metal base while screwing in the bulb.
- To remove a broken bulb from a socket, use a pair of needle-nose pliers to twist the bulb loose. Remember to always disconnect the lamp, or turn off the power at the fuse or circuit breaker. If you don't have a pair of needle-nose pliers handy, press the end of a bar of soap into the broken base, being careful not to cut yourself. Then twist the bar of soap slowly to unscrew the bulb base from the socket.

83 SMALL APPLIANCES

Exercise caution when using small appliances such as toasters or hair dryers. Remember, even small appliances can be dangerous if not used with care.

- Periodically check the power cords on tools or appliances. Replace any cord that is cracked, frayed or gets hot while the gadget is being used.
- Toasters get very hot. Do not hang paper towel racks, towels or curtains where they can be ignited by the toaster.
- To avoid electrical shock, never use a knife or fork to pull bread out of a toaster. If the bread becomes stuck, unplug the toaster and let it cool before using a plastic knife to remove the bread. Be very careful not to damage the heating element when removing bread from a toaster.
- If you feel a tingling shock when you touch an appliance, or detect a burning smell, or the fuse or circuit breaker blows, turn off the power and disconnect the appliance. Have it serviced only by a qualified service center.
- Keep all electrical appliances away from water. Do not use a hair dryer or other corded appliance near water in the bathroom. Don't have a corded radio or TV where it might fall into the bathwater.
- If there are children in the home, insert plastic safety plugs into any unused slots in electrical outlets.
- For shock protection, have a qualified electrician install ground fault circuit interrupters (GFCIs) in any outlet that is near water. This includes kitchen, bath, laundry, garage, and exterior outlets.

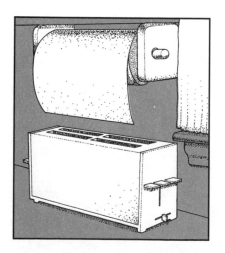

Position the toaster so paper towels and window curtains cannot drape down and catch fire.

84 FURNACE/FLUE MAINTENANCE

For both safety and economy, have your furnace and flue inspected by a professional service person before each heating season begins. Not only will a professional inspection ensure your family's safety, but often a furnace that is properly adjusted can save up to 10 percent on your annual heating bill.

Malfunctioning heating equipment is the third leading cause of fire deaths in the U.S. Heating equipment not only causes fires, but leaky flues can fill the house with dangerous gases such as carbon monoxide. Here is a checklist of things the homeowner can do to keep heating equipment in good operating condition.

- Change furnace filters frequently—at least once per month during peak heating or (if you have central air) cooling seasons. Keeping filters clean will keep your furnace, ducts, and house clean.
- Lubricate blower motor bearings in accordance with the manufacturer's service instructions.
- Vacuum ducts and air registers to keep them free of dirt.
- Each time you change filters, inspect the vent area for clues such as rust or scale. If you note rust, call a service person.

Some maintenance tasks are best left to a service person:

- Check all wiring to be sure it is secure and insulation is intact.
- Check the burner, controls, and thermostat and adjust for proper combustion. Incomplete fuel combustion can cause carbon monoxide buildup.
- Clean and inspect the blower and motor. Also, check the combustion air openings to be sure they are not blocked.
- Check the heat exchanger for rust, holes, or cracks. If the heat exchanger is cracked or rusted out, replace the furnace.
- Check the fuel supply for leaks. Leaking gas or oil can cause a fire or explosion.
- From the roof, check the chimney cap for rust or signs of other damage. Remove the cap and check inside the chimney pipe for bird nests or other debris.

85 EMERGENCY FURNACE OPERATION

Among the controls on a gas-fired, forced-air furnace with a standing pilot light is a tube-shaped device called a thermocouple. The tip of the thermocouple is held in a bracket in the path of the pilot light flame. The heat from the pilot light sends a minicurrent of electrical energy to a gas control valve. As long as the pilot light stays lit, the gas valve stays open and the pilot light has fuel. But if the pilot light goes out, the thermocouple loses that current and the gas valve shuts.

If the pilot light can be lit, but goes out after a burn cycle, suspect a problem with the thermocouple. A service person may have to be summoned to replace the thermocouple. But on a cold day you can repeatedly do a manual lighting to keep the house comfortable until the repair person can get there.

If the pilot light will not stay on, try relighting the pilot light. Instructions for lighting the furnace pilot light usually can be found inside the furnace door. In short, the instructions say to shut off the power, turn down the thermostat, and turn the gas control knob to "off" for a couple of minutes to let the pilot light cool. Turn the control knob to "pilot" position and light

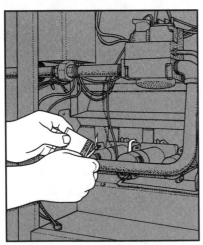

If the furnace pilot will light but won't stay lit after the burn cycle ends, you can maintain comfort in the emergency by lighting the pilot by hand. Repeat the manual lighting as needed to stay warm until the repair person arrives.

the pilot. Now turn the thermostat back up and turn the power on. The burner should ignite. Let the burner and blower complete the burn cycle. Check to see whether the pilot light stays on and whether the burner will ignite with the next call from the thermostat.

If the pilot light goes out, repeat the above process. But, when you turn the thermostat back up, turn it higher than normal, say to 80 degrees Fahrenheit. If, as expected, the pilot goes out again, the house will stay comfortable for an extended time, because you have "superheated" it.

Admittedly, it's a nuisance to have to repeatedly light the pilot light by hand, but it's a much better solution than to simply freeze until the repairman can arrive.

86 BACKUP HEATING SOURCES

If you live in any area where subfreezing winter temperatures are common, by all means you should have an emergency backup heating source. For most homeowners the first backup heat choice is a fireplace. Runners-up in the alternative heating race include wood stoves, pellet stoves that burn fuel pellets made of waste paper or wood, and kerosene- or alcohol-fired portable heaters. All of these choices have their place, but all share a common failing: All are potentially more dangerous, both as fire hazards and as a source of dangerous combustion gases, than furnaces and boilers.

Heater fires are the leading cause of fire death in the southeastern United States. Wood stove fires are a major problem in the northern tier states. The first rule to follow is to read and follow the manufacturer's instructions for safe operation of the equipment.

Burn only seasoned wood. Have the fireplace and chimney cleaned and inspected each fall by pros, and never burn trash in the fireplace. Don't leave a fireplace fire unattended, and never leave young children alone where they might play in the fire. Let the fire burn down near bedtime, bank the fire (at the back of the firebox, put dead ashes on top of live cinders), and be sure the fire screen or glass fire door is closed before going to bed.

The same advice can be followed for wood or pellet stoves. Keep fire intensity within manageable limits; keep the stove and chimney or chimney pipe clean; and place a fireproof surface under the stove to catch any stray embers or sparks. For fireplaces, wood stoves, or any heater that makes ashes, be sure to dispose of ashes safely. Hot ashes dumped outdoors can become windblown sparks that threaten houses and other buildings.

Keep portable kerosene heaters clean, use only approved fuels, and keep the heaters away from combustible furniture, drapes, or wall materials. Unvented combustion gases can be a hazard, especially in today's tighter houses. Open a door or window to freshen the air when you are using a portable heater.

Except in the most dire emergency, do not use gas cookstoves or ovens to heat space. When safety codes were set, gas cooking appliances were exempted from venting requirements on the theory that cooking appliances were used not continuously, i.e., for preparing meals. The unvented gas cooking stoves can become a hazard if used continuously for space heating. Even when cooking holiday or other multicourse meals on an unvented gas range, exhaust fans should be used and supplemental ventilation provided by opening doors or windows.

CHAPTER SEVEN

125

REMOVING BARRIERS FOR THE ELDERLY

TIPS

87 ELDER ALERT

Do you or any senior family member have any special medical or physical problems of which emergency or rescue workers should be aware? If the answer to that question is yes, consider joining Elder Alert, a program designed to ensure the safety of senior citizens.

How the program works: The senior citizen is given an Elder Alert Protection System kit that includes a bright orange plastic emergency tube, an emergency medical information sheet, and an Elder Alert Protection System sticker. The senior citizen fills out the medical information sheet, listing any pertinent health information. The senior then inserts the medical information sheet into the plastic emergency tube, and then places the emergency tube in the refrigerator. Then the Elder Alert sticker is placed on the refrigerator door.

If emergency workers such as fire or medical rescue teams are summoned to the home, they immediately check the refrigerator door to look for the Elder Alert System Sticker. If workers see the sticker, they retrieve the emergency tube and medical information from inside the refrigerator, and take appropriate medical action. The Elder Alert System is a trademark of NovaCare, Inc., a national provider of health services. To find out if there is an Elder Alert program in your community, or to help start the service in your area, call 800-395-5000.

Make a list of your medical history, including chronic conditions, medications, and personal physicians, and place the list in the Elder Alert tube. Place the tube in plain view inside the refrigerator where emergency crews will look for it.

88 BURN PREVENTION

It is best if the elderly do not perform cooking chores. The elderly family member may have increasing problems with balance, or may be unsure of foot. At the same time, he may also have poor circulation, which can reduce the sense of touch and pain, and may suffer deep burns without being aware of it. Also, because of the danger of spillage, the server should allow hot food or beverages to cool slightly before serving them to those with impaired mobility.

Seniors who continue to cook should avoid wearing loose clothing, such as robes or housecoats, around the stove. Loose clothing can catch on hot pots or pans, spilling the contents, or may dangle against a hot burner and catch fire. Most kitchen fires occur when burners are left unattended under cooking food. Always turn off the burner first before you remove a pot or pan from it, and turn off the burner under cooking food before leaving the kitchen.

Senior citizens should be especially careful to never smoke in bed, and should never leave any room before extinguishing smoking materials. When using a clothes iron, turn the iron off and unplug it if you must leave the area.

To avoid scalds, turn down the water heater thermostat to 120 degrees Fahrenheit or less. If set above 130 degrees Fahrenheit, the hot water can cause third-degree burns (most severe) in two seconds. When drawing a bath, always turn on cold water first, then slowly add hot water. Before climbing into the bath, test the bathwater temperature with a thermometer or the elbow.

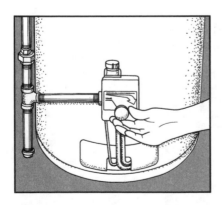

Prevent scalding injuries to children and others by turning down the thermostat on a hot water heater. Hot water running to home taps should be set to no more than 120 degrees Fahrenheit.

89 FIRE SAFETY FOR SENIORS

Seniors are at the highest risk of being killed in a fire: They die in fires at twice the national rate. Because they may be less alert or less mobile, seniors should have their own checklist for fire safety. Consider this sample checklist:

- Install a smoke alarm in the hall outside the bedroom door, or in the bedroom proper. For the hearing impaired, buy a smoke alarm that combines the audible feature with a flashing strobe light, and install it in the bedroom rather than in a hall.
- Keep three things by the senior's bed: the phone, a loud police whistle, and eyeglasses. The senior will need his glasses to be able to see the escape route, and a police whistle can be used to summon help or to alert fire fighters that he is still in his room.
- The entire family, including seniors, should participate in family fire drills. If the senior uses a wheelchair or walker, check the escape route in advance to be sure the route is adequate for passage.
- Do not try to retrieve memorabilia or valuables. To do so may cost precious seconds of escape time. Get out of the house.
- At the sound of the alarm, or if you smell smoke, drop out of bed and crawl to the door. If the door feels hot to the touch, do not open the door, because smoke or fire might enter the room.
- If you must remain in the room during a fire, use towels or clothing to plug the crack under the door. To help you breathe in smoke, cover your mouth and nose with a (wet) pillowcase or handkerchief. Hang a sheet

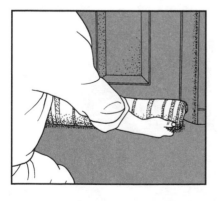

If you must remain in the room during a fire, use a wet towel or rolled-up rag to plug the crack under the door to keep out heat and smoke.

or blanket out the window to let the fire fighters know you are in the room.

- In major metropolitan areas fire response time may be five minutes or less. Check with the fire department to know in advance the average fire fighter response time to your home or apartment. If you live in an urban area and fire fighters are nearby, don't panic. Help will arrive. Don't jump from a high window unless the fire and smoke actually threaten to overcome you.

90 FIRE SAFETY FOR TRAVELERS

Most retirees love to travel, but fire safety in a hotel or motel may be a concern. Most public facilities are required by fire codes to have room smoke alarms, fire sprinkler systems, and well-marked exits. Still, for your own safety and peace of mind, familiarize yourself with the fire security and escape avenues from your particular hotel or motel.

- When making travel plans, inquire about the fire security of a particular motel/hotel chain. If you are impressed by the fire security efforts of one particular chain, make all your trip reservations at that chain's facilities.
- When packing for a trip, always put a small flashlight and spare batteries in your luggage. Pack a night-light and use it in strange rooms to help orient yourself in an emergency.
- When you check into your room, first test the smoke alarm to be sure it is working. If the test button does not cause an alarm to sound, call the front desk and ask that the alarm be serviced.
- Locate the fire alarm on your door. Sound the alarm if you detect a fire problem in any part of the building.
- Identify two exit paths out of the building. In case you must feel your way through a smoke-filled hall, count down the number of room doors between your room and the exit door.
- Learn the layout of your room or suite and know how to unlock the door in the dark.
- Place your room key and a flashlight by your bed. If the fire alarm sounds in the night, take only your key and flashlight with you.
- If you hear any alarm in the night, act immediately to get out of the building.
- If you leave the room, close the door behind you. Open doors help create drafts and spread the fire through the building.
- If the hall is on fire, call room service and tell them you are trapped. To keep out smoke, use wet towels to block gaps under or around the door. Wet a towel or pillowcase and hold it over your mouth and nose to help you breathe.
- In case of fire, never use the elevator. It may stop at the fire floor or the electrical service may be disrupted and trap you between floors. In a fire, use the stairs.
- Remember, about half of hotel fires are caused by careless smoking.
- Also, shop department stores for room security devices such as lock alarms or auxiliary door locks to keep out intruders.

91 CAR SAFETY FOR SENIORS

Of all life's hazards, car crashes are the most common cause of accidental death. Although the accidental death rate slows a bit for seniors, car accidents are the leading killer for people between the ages of 1 and 44. To ensure happy trails, seniors should follow these safe driving tips:

- Keep your car in good shape. Have equipment such as brakes, tires, windshield washers and wipers, and exhaust system serviced frequently to be sure the car is roadworthy.
- Have your eyes checked annually. Wear sunglasses to protect your vision in sunlight, and avoid driving at night if night vision becomes troublesome.
- Local senior services may offer brush-up classes in drivers' training. To be sure your driving is safe for today's traffic, attend one of these classes. Check with your auto insurance agent. Many companies offer insurance discounts to seniors who take brush-up driving classes.
- Don't drive when you are tired. Don't drive at night in unfamiliar territory. Plan to be off the roads before dark.
- Use your seat belts. Good drivers are killed by bad drivers, so don't count on your own driving skills to save you. Ask all passengers in the car to use the belts; it's good training for young and old alike, and seat belts have been shown to be effective in reducing death and injuries.
- If you are shopping for a new car, choose one that has air bags and the automatic braking system (ABS). Automatic brakes prevent wheels from locking up and skidding during a panic stop.

92 TIPS FOR THE HANDICAPPED

People who have physical limitations or use wheelchairs should make special emergency preparations. Whether the emergency is a storm, an earthquake, or a fire, making special provisions in advance can help ensure survival.

- For emergency use, the blind or visually impaired should store extra canes along a planned evacuation route.
- If the blind person has a seeing-eye dog, he should store extra pet food to be used in an emergency.
- The person who uses a wheelchair should have a drawstring bag attached to the chair. The bag can hold special medications, a small flashlight, and a police whistle to be used to summon aid.
- Be sure the handicapped evacuation route will permit a wheelchair to exit.
- For emergency insurance, have a buddy system. Agree with a neighbor, friend, or family member to look out for each other if problems arise.
- Make a list of medical information, including allergies and needed medicines, and a list of addresses and phone numbers for your physician, pharmacist, close friends, and next of kin. Keep a copy (see Elder Alert, p. 123), and give a copy to each person in your buddy system.
- For use when electrical power is interrupted, install emergency nightlights with battery backup power.
- Store at least a three-day emergency supply of any special medicines or dietary items.
- If a person uses a wheelchair the rules are as follows: Stay in the chair. Move out of danger if possible. If you are in a storm or earthquake, move to the safest part of the house. Lock your wheels and protect your head by covering up with a lap robe, books, or your arms. Have the police whistle handy and blow it periodically to alert searchers where you are.

93 BARRIER-FREE KITCHENS

Whether building new or remodeling, you can make the kitchen barrier-free for handicapped or elderly family members. Consider these tips when making your kitchen more accessible:

- Install a single-lever kitchen faucet. Having the single lever lets you control both water volume and temperature using only a closed hand or even an elbow.
- To aid people with a diminished hand grip, replace pull-knob cabinet door or drawer hardware with D-shaped pull handles.
- To aid those with impaired vision, install bright task lighting over the sink and cooktop areas.
- Hot spills and burns can occur when a person misses a countertop while setting down a hot pan. Be sure countertops and vinyl floor covering are in contrasting colors, so the edge of the countertop stands out clearly against the floor covering.
- To avoid having to reach over a hot front burner to reach a back burner, buy a cooktop with offset front and back burners.
- A side-by-side refrigerator/freezer is the most accessible style for a cook who is seated in a wheelchair.

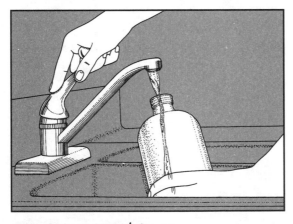

A single-lever kitchen faucet controls both water temperature and volume, and is easy for elderly or infirm to use.

94 BARRIER-FREE BATHROOMS

The bathroom is the most dangerous room in the house, and is especially hazardous to those with reduced mobility. Here are tips for making your bathroom barrier-free.

- For good visibility and to avoid mistakes in reading or taking prescriptions, install bright lighting in the bathroom. For good visibility seniors who are over seventy years old may require three times as much light as a person who is in his twenties.
- To avoid bathtub or shower falls, install grab bars. Grab bars can be attached to the walls (must be attached to wood framing) or can be attached to the front edge of the tub.
- If a person is unsteady on foot, add a seat to the bathtub. Shop for tub seats and grab bars at hospital supply stores.
- If you are replacing a bathtub or adding a shower, shop your plumbing supplier for new shower stalls that are wheelchair accessible.
- To keep medicines separate and to avoid mistakes in medication, senior couples should install his and hers medicine cabinets.
- Dispose of outdated prescription drugs by flushing them down the toilet. Keeping outdated drugs about can lead to mistakes in medication.
- If you drop a pill or capsule in the bathroom, dispose of it. Never pick up and ingest any pill from the floor. The pill you are taking may not be the one you dropped.

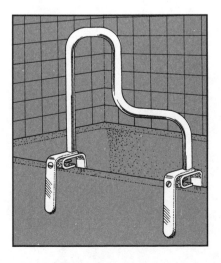

A grip rail such as this one will help seniors get in and out of the tub without slipping.

95 INDOOR AIR QUALITY

Many seniors who live in cold climates, uncomfortable in the cold and fearful of falling on icy walks, may restrict their movements in winter. Because of advanced age and reduced circulation, these folks may chill easily, so to keep out drafts they block cracks around doors or windows with rags or with small rugs. To avoid dangerous falls they may also refuse to go out in snowy weather, so exterior doors are seldom opened and fresh air cannot enter. If a forced air furnace in a closed-up house cannot draw in fresh combustion air, the furnace may back-draft or draw combustion gases back into the house, and a dangerous carbon monoxide buildup may occur. The result is that air quality in a senior's home may suffer, and may even become dangerous.

Remember also that gas cooking stoves are not vented. This may not pose a problem when one is cooking ordinary meals and burners may be on for only a short time. But when making a holiday dinner, or when the oven and stovetop burners are all on for an extended period, combustion gas buildup may be a hazard. Be sure to run the hood exhaust fan or open a nearby window to remove dangerous gases.

One solution for better air quality is to open up the house frequently, throwing doors and windows open to air out the house. If a family member cannot comfortably bear the brief exposure to cold, shut off one room to shelter that person, air out the rest of the house, then let the house warm before opening the door to that one room.

96 EXTERIOR SECURITY

There are things you can do to make your house exterior both more accessible and also more secure. Consider adding these options:

- A garage door opener can open the garage door and turn on the light without your having to leave the car. These are especially welcome features when you return home alone, during a rain- or snowstorm, or very late at night.
- Cut away or trim any shrubbery that blocks visibility at house entrances. Shrubbery can conceal a prowler or mugger.
- Install motion detector lights at all outside entrance doors. These lights will greet arriving guests, warn intruders, and provide security lighting for you or your family.
- Install dead bolt locks on all entrance doors.
- Buy a phone message recorder. Burglars often call a target home from a pay phone or car phone and listen at the house for the phone to quit ringing. If the phone continues to ring, they assume no one is home, and break in. The phone message recorder will stop ringing after a brief period so burglar is unsure whether (1) you did not pick up the phone or (2) you have returned home.

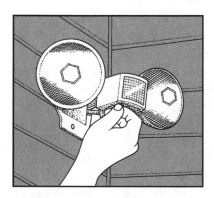

A motion detector light at each entry door can be a welcome beacon in the night, and a powerful deterrent to prowlers.

97 AVOIDING BURGLARS

Leaving your house for a vacation may make it an inviting target for burglars. Families that have multiple breadwinners leave the house unoccupied for hours at a time on a daily basis, inviting daytime burglars. And Christmas holidays invite thieves to take their pick of the gifts under the tree. Here are things you can do to take that bull's-eye off your front door and make your house a less inviting target.

- Always leave your phone answering machine turned on, but don't leave a "We're on vacation" message to advise burglars of a long absence. Choose a simple "We can't come to the phone now" message and don't alter it when you go away on vacation.
- When you buy expensive appliances, don't leave the packing boxes by the curb to be picked up with the trash. Those boxes are like a neon sign that tells burglars, "The Smiths have a new TV. And a VCR. And a new CD player. . . . " The same is true for Christmas gift boxes left in the trash. Cut the boxes in small pieces and place the pieces in plastic trash bags. Or cut the tape on cardboard box seams and flatten the boxes so they don't advertise what's new with you.
- Notify your local police when you will be away for vacation. Also, set up a neighborhood watch program so neighbors look out for each other.
- Ask a neighbor to park his car in your drive in your absence.
- Cancel mail delivery. Call your newspaper to cancel deliveries.
- If you live in a wealthy suburb, if your house is set back from the street, or if you have a curbside mailbox and no one is home during the day, you are a most likely target for a burglar.
- Pick up delivered mail quickly. Don't leave mail uncollected in a curbside mailbox. It is easy for a drive-by burglar to check your mail while "casing" your house. By checking your mail he knows, among other facts, your name, whether you have a charge card, your bank account number, and the name of your stockbroker.
- Have the lawn mowed in your absence. Also, snow that is unshoveled and untracked proves there has been no activity at your house.
- Install motion detector lights at all entry doors. Install timers on radios, lights, or TV sets so there is random noise and light activity from the house. Buy lamps that are sound-activated, and place them near likely break-in points.
- Record on audio tape an evening's family activity and plug the tape player into a timer that will play the tape in your absence.

98 PERSONAL SECURITY

Today there is a growing concern in this country over the increasingly mean streets. In many cities there is a general feeling that it simply is not safe to be about, even in daylight. Self-defense classes are springing up, and thousands of people are buying handguns for self-defense. What can the average person do to ensure personal security? First, most experts agree that everyone should know basic self-defense, i.e., study karate or other martial arts. But experts also agree that there is little chance that the average 120-pound woman is going to physically dominate a 200-pound mugger. Pros know the old bettor's adage: In a fight a good big man will beat a good little man (or woman).

Whether we are talking about karate or handguns, self-defense ultimately boils down to one point: To successfully beat a mugger at his own game, you must not only have the ability to hurt the attacker, but you must also be willing, even eager, to do so. Could you really shoot another person? If you choose to carry any weapon, use it decisively. If you hesitate, the attacker will use the weapon on you. For the less aggressive among us, it is far better to develop street smarts than to study karate. This means we will face reality and avoid situations that will lead to confrontation. Here are some tips to keep in mind:

- A stalled car that strands you in a remote or crime area invites confrontation. Keep your car in top operating condition. In most cases car trouble can be averted by regular maintenance. Worn tires, batteries or fan belts, dirty radiators, and an engine needing a tune-up are minor repairs that through neglect become expensive emergencies.
- Drive with car doors locked.
- If you are approached by an armed carjacker, don't resist. Give him your car. Check out new security devices that permit a carjacker to drive your car a short way, but will then shut off the electrical system.
- Don't go out alone at night.
- If you do go out, stay with the crowds.
- When you go out, advise someone of your destination and your estimated return time. Be time-conscious and always prompt. Alarms are not sent out for undependable or chronically late people.
- Park in an attended parking lot or ramp.
- If you must park on a public street, park under a street light. Do not leave personal property in view. Lock it in the trunk or leave it home. Lock your car.

135

- While in public, carry a whistle or alarm in your hand, ready to use.
- Be aware of what's happening around you. Keep scanning about to spot potential problems and to decide on an escape route if a problem develops. Walk at curbside to avoid passing close to a dark alley.
- Choose a new car with security options. Some models have light delay switches that leave lights burning until you are inside the place of destination. Some cars have remote controls that permit you to turn on the car's interior lights from a distance, so you can check the interior for intruders. Aftermarket remote lights can be purchased for any car.
- Carry a money clip with a $20 bill outside and a handful of small bills in the center. Keep the money clip handy, in your pocket or purse. If you are approached by a mugger, scream, and throw the money clip away. When the mugger goes for the clip, take off running in the opposite direction.
- If a mugger has got you cornered, give him whatever he wants. Fight only as a last resort, when you feel your life is threatened.

CHAPTER EIGHT

125

STORMS AND NATURAL DISASTERS

TIPS

99 HOME INSURANCE

Your insurance agent is the best source of information here. Some natural disasters are fully covered under homeowner insurance (tornadoes, hail damage), while earthquake or flood damage may require extra coverage. Be sure your house insurance coverage is up-to-date, because the inflation of past years has resulted in rapid increases in the cost of both house construction and furnishings. Be sure the insurance on the house and all your personal possessions reflect their current value.

In addition to insuring the house and furnishings, be aware that there are limits on ordinary coverage of expensive items such as jewelry, furs, cameras, guns, and collections. For example, unless you have bought a rider for extra coverage, a typical household policy may pay a maximum of a thousand dollars for lost jewelry or camera equipment. If you collect expensive jewelry or furs, keep receipts for each item that you buy, and have an expert (jeweler or furrier) appraise your present collection. Take these written appraisals to your insurance agent and have him attach a rider to your policy, extending coverage to the extra items.

Other overlooked items may include your electronic gear. Stereos, VCRs, computers, and gadget-laden home phones can represent a large investment, so have your insurance coverage extended to reflect the true value of all your furnishings and personal property.

100 PROOF OF LOSS

If the total contents of your home were lost in a disaster such as a fire or a tornado, could you prove ownership of every item you lost? Or, in the aftermath of such an emergency, could you even remember to list every item? To be sure you will be fully compensated for every item lost, make a checklist, and also keep a photographic record of your personal property.

First, make a comprehensive written checklist of all your household possessions. Where possible, include the brand name or make and model of every appliance, camera, or piece of electronic gear. Open clothes closets and make a count of clothing items. List all suits, topcoats, furs, and sports gear.

As mentioned above (see Home Insurance, p. 139), get expert written appraisals for valuable items, including jewelry, furs, guns, and other expensive sports equipment. Make multiple copies of the appraisals so you have copies available both for your insurance agent and also for your own records.

Use a quality still or video camera to make a photo record of each room. Be sure that every item of value that you own is clearly displayed in the photos. Take extra photos as needed to be sure everything of value is shown. Open closet doors and photograph the entire contents, because even a modest wardrobe can add up to a replacement cost of several thousand dollars.

Make several copies of the photos or videotapes. Keep one set of photo records at home, in your own files. You should also keep backup records in case your home records are lost or destroyed. At the home of a relative or in a safety deposit box, keep a full set of records, including both photos and written checklists.

101 CONTRACTOR/REPAIR RIP-OFFS

It's difficult to believe that there are people who will try to capitalize on human misery, but some rip-off artists specialize in taking advantage of the afflicted, and victims of natural disasters are their chosen prey. These unscrupulous contractors may show up on your doorstep and try to take advantage of your pain and confusion. They will also stress their immediate availability, a sure lure at a time of wide destruction, when contractors' services will be in increased demand.

The first precaution is to be aware that much of the damage to your house may be difficult to see. For example, earthquakes can break and distort foundations and footings. Earthquakes or windstorms can twist a building so it is out of plumb and square. The damage to the house may appear to the amateur to be cosmetic, with cracked plaster and splintered trim, when in fact an architect or building engineer might condemn the building as beyond repair.

An unscrupulous contractor might make superficial repairs and disappear with your bank account, leaving you to face the financial music. Don't rush into a repair contract because of a sense of urgency over the situation.

Check any contractor's credentials to be sure his company is local and that he can provide both financial and job references. Check out all references offered, because the rip-off artist will have a fraudulent list. Be sure the contractor has met any city requirements for licensing, bonding, and insurance. Get at least three bids and choose carefully who you will work with.

Get everything in writing. This includes the description of the job, agreed dates for starting and finishing the project, a material specifications sheet that includes the make, model, and/or type of materials that will be used, plus the contractor's license number and insurance certificate. Be sure every detail of the agreement is included in the written contract.

In a stressful time, remember that you are in charge, and it is your money at stake. Don't advance the contractor a large sum up front. Make a reasonable down payment and spell out in writing exactly how the balance of the money will be paid as materials are delivered and work progresses.

102 CAR EMERGENCIES

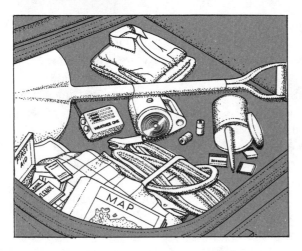

An emergency kit for the car should include a good road map, a pair of blankets, weather radio, flashlight and spare batteries, jumper cables, matches and candles in a waterproof metal can, a first aid kit, and shovel.

If you have an opportunity or orders from authorities to leave a distress area, be sure your car is dependable and properly maintained to make the trip. Read and follow the owner's manual for the car, and have all the services performed at recommended intervals. This means keeping clean oil and antifreeze in the car, keeping it tuned, and replacing tires, radiator hoses, and belts before they fail. Keep the gas tank full when storms threaten and you know you may be forced to flee.

In addition to maintaining the car in good condition, you should keep emergency items in the car. Some items to include in your emergency kit will depend on the type of emergency for which you are preparing, and these special items will be listed for each emergency, but a basic list belongs in every car. This list includes road maps, a portable radio, flashlight and extra batteries, jumper cables, one or more blankets or sleeping bags, and a first aid kit. Also, keep in the car a bright cloth (to be waved or tied to the car radio antenna) or a SEND POLICE sign to display on the windshield or a back window. And a cellular telephone is a real safety item in any emergency situation.

103 SHUT OFF HOUSE UTILITIES

With a storm or other disaster approaching, you've made the decision to leave your house. What steps can you take to try to limit damage to the house and contents in your absence? First, turn off all standing pilot lights and shut off all utilities. Locate (or ask your utility company to locate for you) all these shutoff valves so you and other family members know where they are and how to shut them off. You may wish to borrow a tip from industry and use an aerosol spray paint to paint all utility shutoff valves or fuses bright white to make them easy to locate and identify.

To avoid electrical fires or deadly shock in a house that may be subject to storm damage, pull the main fuse (at the main entry panel) to shut down all electrical circuits in the house. Turn the gate valve (on the water supply pipe, on the street side of the water meter) to shut off city water.

If you have a water well, shut off the valve at the top of the well pump, or on the supply pipe from the well to the house. Experts advise not to shut off the gas in earthquakes until after the quake has stopped, and then only if you smell gas. To prevent a gas fire or an explosion, shut off the natural gas at the meter. Most shutoff valves require use of a wrench to shut off the gas service. To avoid having to look for a wrench during an emergency, buy one of the right size and use clothes hanger wire to hang it near the shutoff valve. If you have to shut off the gas, there may be leaks that have not yet been repaired. For safety, have a professional serviceman check to be sure everything is in working order and let him turn the gas back on.

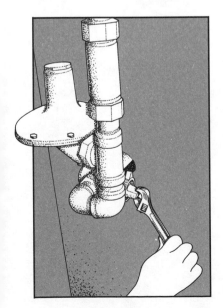

Electricity and water shutoffs can be done by hand. For emergency use, keep a wrench by the gas meter/shutoff. Each family member should know the location of utility shutoff valves.

104 FLOODS

If you must evacuate in anticipation of a flood, shut off all utilities. Then, check to be sure your car is gassed up and the emergency kit is in your car. Use the car or other battery-powered radio to monitor media and government bulletins regarding the timing of potential dangers and recommended evacuation routes.

If time permits, move all furniture and personal belongings to upper floors. If you cannot move everything to a higher area, then stack the most valuable or expensive items on the tallest tables or highest shelves to try and keep them out of the water. Disconnect the power plug on large appliances that cannot be moved, such as a refrigerator or range.

The most important thing to do is to keep a weather eye out and move to higher ground ahead of the flood. Family safety is more important than material possessions. Don't wait until water covers and conceals the pathway to safety. Don't try to wade or drive through standing water where no bottom is visible. Roads or driveways can wash out in a flood and water may be deeper than it appears. Also, it is easy to misjudge the force of currents when flood waters are raging, and the car may be forced from the road by the current. The best bet is to head for high ground while you can still see your exit route.

105 CLEANING FLOOD-DAMAGED APPLIANCES

When returning to a house that has been flooded, have a professional electrician check all house wiring and appliances before you attempt to replace the main fuse or use the service. Switches and other electrical devices that have been flooded can be wet and can short out or cause dangerous shock to a family member. Light fixtures and lamps should be removed, dissassembled, and cleaned before use. Replace the power cords on floor or table lamps.

Major appliances such as the refrigerator and freezer have sealed motors and may survive a flood without damage. However, appliance wiring and electrical components such as relays and thermostats should be checked by an electrician. For appliances that have motors, such as saws, hair dryers, blenders, or food processors, remove the motors and take them to an appliance repair shop. All electric motors should be cleaned and dried before use.

Sewing machines also need attention if subjected to flood waters. Remove the motor and take it to an appliance repair shop to have it cleaned and dried. Clean the sewing head with solvent. Soak any affected parts in kerosene, wipe them dry, and then coat with a light film of oil.

106 CLEANING FLOOD-DAMAGED INTERIORS

Flood waters can leave your home's interior and furnishings a sodden mess. But fighting a house fire can also cause widespread water damage, so most of the advice for dealing with flood-damaged materials applies not only to floods, but also to water damage inflicted by fire fighters.

Floors with vinyl or linoleum coverings can be damaged when water seeps between the floor plywood underlayment and the coverings. Either delamination or separation of the ply layers and/or a moldy or mildew smell may result. The trapped water cannot dry out until the floor covering is removed. After the floor underlayment has dried, replace the floor covering.

Water that seeps underneath floor covering may not ruin the entire covering, but can cause patchy areas where the floor covering adhesive fails and small blisters occur in the covering. Sometimes the small blisters can be repaired by slitting the blister and injecting floor covering adhesive into the blistered area. This repair is best done by a pro.

Water or steam can ruin locks and hinges. They should be taken apart, wiped dry, and coated with a lubricant before being reassembled.

Dirty or smoked walls and ceilings can be cleaned by mixing five tablespoons of trisodium phosphate (TSP, from your paint store) with one cup of bleach, into one gallon of warm water. Wash affected surfaces and let dry by providing plenty of natural ventilation. To increase the air flow and reduce drying time, remove screens from windows and use portable house fans. Don't be in a hurry to repaint. A new paint coat can seal moisture in walls or ceilings, causing mold or mildew and odors to develop in the wall cavities. Wait to repaint until walls or ceilings are completely dry.

Remove and disassemble locks. Clean and dry the lock, then apply a thin film of lubricant.

107 CLEANING FLOOD-DAMAGED FURNITURE

Because of the padding or fill, smoke and mildew odors are difficult to remove from pillows, mattresses, and upholstered furniture. These items usually must be discarded after a fire or flood. In an emergency you may be able to use a mattress temporarily by leaving the mattress to dry in the sun, then covering it with plastic sheeting.

Furniture items made of particle board or plywood may be permanently damaged by water exposure. By careful treatment solid wood furniture can often be salvaged. Follow these steps:

- Use warm water, a mild detergent, and stiff brush to wash away any mud or dirt.
- Remove doors and drawers from cabinets or dressers, and set them apart to dry. This will allow full air circulation to dry the wood, and help ensure that the doors and drawers won't stick in the future.
- Dry wood items slowly. Do not leave water-soaked wood furniture to dry in direct sunlight, because too much heat may warp and twist the wood.
- Keep the wood furniture in the shade, preferably indoors with doors and windows open for ventilation. Running a dehumidifier may help.
- Remove any mold with borax dissolved in hot water (see label on borax for proper mix proportion).
- White spots or film may develop on the wood finish. Mix ½ cup household ammonia with ½ cup warm water, and use a clean cloth to wipe this solution over the white areas. Let the wood dry.
- When the wood is dry, use 4/0 (fine) steel wool to apply a liquid polishing wax. Buff the wax with a soft cloth.

108 WEATHER RADIOS

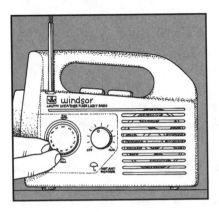

For an emergency radio, choose a sportsman's model that combines weather, AM and FM radio, plus a powerful flashlight. Keep a spare set of batteries with the radio.

The National Oceanic and Atmospheric Administration (NOAA) and National Weather Service are divisions within the U.S. Department of Commerce. NOAA Weather Radio operates about 375 radio stations, broadcasting 24 hours a day, and 90 percent of the U.S. population is within listening range of a NOAA Weather Radio broadcast.

On weather radio, taped weather messages are repeated every four to six minutes and are routinely updated throughout the day. Also, NOAA personnel can interrupt taped weather broadcasts during severe weather to alert the audience to vital warning information. These emergency messages may inform the audience of tornadoes, severe thunderstorms, flash flood warnings or watches, and hurricanes.

In addition to emergency broadcasts NOAA also forecasts weather developments of interest to farmers, travelers, boaters, fishermen, and other recreational pursuits. Weather updates may include temperatures, precipitation, flooding, and Coast Guard reports for both coastal and inland waterways.

Weather radios operate on FM marine band frequencies that are not found on the average home radio. These high frequencies are between 162.40 and 162.55 megahertz. A number of manufacturers make weather radios that operate on these frequencies. Some of the radios are called "warning alarm receivers" and have an alarm that can be activated by the NOAA in case of impending disasters. If you live in an area where storms are frequent, or engage in an occupation or recreation that is dependent on the weather, buy one of these weather radios. Weather radios are available with or without the warning alarms, and radio prices range between $15 and $50. The radios are available from Radio Shack or other electronic stores.

109 UNDERSTANDING WEATHER TERMS

When storm conditions exist, the weather stations use terms such as "severe thunderstorm watch" or "severe thunderstorm warning." What do these terms mean? To be prepared for any eventuality we should understand all the terms used in forecasting severe weather.

A *severe thunderstorm watch* means that weather conditions exist that may produce heavy rain, hail, lightning, damaging winds, or even tornadoes. Take primary emergency precautions and use good judgment as you travel or move about. Be prepared to take appropriate shelter.

A *severe thunderstorm warning* means that weather officials have reports of thunderstorm sightings or movement on weather radar. Follow weather news broadcasts for further advisory information. Any combination of rain, hail, wind, lightning, or tornadoes is possible. Travel only in an emergency and be prepared to go to shelter.

A *tornado watch* means that the weather conditions necessary to produce a tornado (or severe thunderstorm) are present. These include warm, humid air, rapidly rising air, an upper-level jet stream (zone of high-speed wind), and a low-pressure area or storm front. Stay tuned to weather station for breaking developments.

A *tornado warning* means that a tornado funnel has actually been sighted. In many metropolitan areas emergency sirens will sound with a steady blast for three to five minutes. Take a battery-powered radio with you as you head to shelter. Do not come out of the shelter area until the "all clear" has been announced.

Similar weather forecasts can warn of other storms. For example, because they are spawned over water, hurricanes can be detected and tracked far in advance of actual landfall. Hurricane Andrew presented his calling card four days in advance of actually reaching land, providing ample time for evacuation or emergency measures. Modern weather equipment is such that it not only can detect the formation of a hurricane, but can even forecast the severity of the approaching storm.

110 HURRICANES AND TORNADOES

Broken windows and flying glass are major hazards in violent storms. If you live in an area that is subject to frequent windstorms, consider building plywood shutters in advance, to cover windows as predicted storms approach. Plywood window shutters can be predrilled for drywall screws, and a cordless screwdriver and a handful of screws will help you cover the windows in a matter of a few minutes. If you don't have plywood shutters, keep a roll of tough duct tape on hand and place two strips of duct tape in an X pattern on the window glass. If window glass is shattered during a storm, the duct tape will prevent the glass from flying and injuring house occupants. To shatterproof large glass panes in patio doors or picture windows, apply extra strips of duct tape to the glass. Or have the glass covered with the new tough plastic films.

Often, much of the property damage and human injuries caused by windstorms are the result of lawn and garden items that become airborne in the blast. Keep trash cans inside a garage, or use a small chain to secure the cans to a sturdy anchor such as a tree or well-anchored fence post. Bring children's toys and patio furniture into a garage so they are sheltered from the wind. Consider the potential damage to your house from windblown shade trees, and have trees that are near the house pruned or removed if your tree expert decides they are a threat to the house. Remember that any yard or garden structure that is not well-anchored can become windblown and represents a potential hazard.

As any type of windstorm approaches, move the family to the lowest level of the house—the basement if you have one, or a first floor. Move to a hallway or central area of the house, away from windows and doors.

Don't attempt to go outside until authorities sound the all clear and you are sure the storm is over. Remember that there is a quiet center or "eye" in a hurricane, so that the storm passes over in two phases. There have also been reports that tornadoes have hit in two stages, indicating that either the storm turned or more than one funnel passed over.

Be aware that any downed power lines may be live or hot and may present a shock threat over a large area of wet ground, so stay well away from any downed power lines.

If you are outside when a windstorm hits and you don't have time to move indoors, lie facedown in a ditch, with your hands over your head. This position will help you avoid head injuries from flying objects.

If you are driving when a tornado approaches, stop the car and try to move indoors to safety. If you cannot reach shelter, get out of the car and lie down in a ditch as above. If you live in a manufactured (mobile) home park, your dealer can use steel cables to tie down the home. Most mobile home parks provide a storm shelter of some sort, usually found in a masonry laundry or utility building. Check where the park shelter is, and move to the shelter when tornadoes are forecast. If your mobile home is on a private lot, plan in advance where your family can find shelter in a storm emergency.

 **MAKING YOUR HOUSE EARTHQUAKE-RESISTANT**

California has the highest earthquake risk of any state in the contiguous 48 states, and has experienced quakes with a magnitude of 8.3 on the Richter scale (the 1906 San Francisco quake). That record has never been equalled since, but earthquakes with magnitudes of 6.5 or greater occur every four years in California, with extensive damage to real property. However, architects and building engineers have found that well-built houses, especially those houses built since earthquake building codes were adopted, can withstand severe quakes without major structural damage. If you are shopping for a house, remember that its resistance to earthquake damage depends on its age, design, and quality of construction. If you are house shopping, it is a good investment to have the house evaluated for its ability to withstand an earthquake by an architect or building engineer.

It is also agreed by architects and engineers that most existing houses can be reinforced to be more earthquake resistant. Hire an architect or builder to evaluate your house and to estimate the cost of implementing necessary measures to make the house more resistant to quakes.

First, check the foundation to be sure the wooden sill plate is anchored via anchor bolts to the concrete foundation. Next, if your house is built on a cripple wall or wood foundation, reinforce the cripple wall with sheathing plywood and/or backing blocks.

If you have a room built over a garage, the wide span of the garage door header is a structural weak spot and can collapse during a quake. Plywood panels can brace wood frame walls against quake stresses. Using drywall screws, install plywood sheathing inside the garage, on the walls next to the door opening.

Exterior portions of the house may collapse during an earthquake. Have house additions such as porches, balconies, or overhangs checked by an engineer or contractor to be sure they are adequately supported and attached to the house. Heavy roof materials such as slate or tile may loosen and fall during an earthquake. Also, a heavy roof can cause a "whiplash" effect that can add force to an earthquake's vibration and can cause or contribute to structural damage to the house. Have a roofing contractor inspect your slate or tile roof to be sure it is in good shape. If you are building or remodeling, consider choosing a lighter roofing material such as asphalt shingles.

A weak fireplace chimney can collapse during an earthquake. Older chimneys, especially those built before 1934, are most vulnerable to collapse. If your house has a chimney that extends far above the roof, or one that stands next to an exterior wall, have the chimney checked by a structural engineer. If an earthquake has occurred, have your fireplace chimney checked for cracks before lighting a fire in it. Have pros check out any large, leaning, or old trees that are near the house and might fall in an earthquake. Remove any large dead limbs or even the entire tree if it presents a hazard to the house.

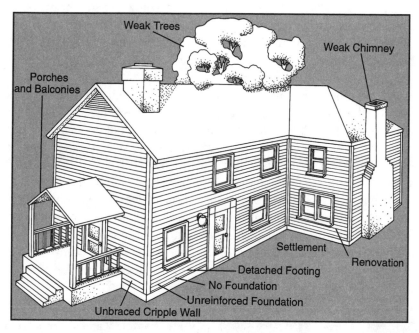

Exterior Earthquake Hazards

SECURE THE HOUSE
INTERIOR AGAINST QUAKES

To minimize damage to the house and to prevent injury to the occupants, do a complete inspection of your home's interior furnishings. Avoid having tall, freestanding furniture or appliances that might topple in an earthquake or storm. To secure heavy furniture from falling, screw or strap heavy objects to wall framing.

Move your bed and favorite chair away from windows or heavy furniture that might topple. Do not hang mirrors or heavy pictures over the bed or chair in such a way that they might fall on you.

If you are in an earthquake or hurricane zone, avoid having hanging plants or pots and pans on open racks. Also, avoid heavy glass chandeliers or ceiling fans that might break free during an emergency and fall on you.

Anchor china cabinets, TV sets, refrigerators, bookcases, clocks, pictures, or mirrors to the walls. Store heavy items on the floor or on the lowest shelves, close to the floor, so they won't have far to fall in an emergency.

If you remodel the house, be sure your project does not weaken the house structure. For example, do not remove small windows to install large windows or window walls. Although load-bearing walls are sometimes removed and replaced by a support beam, do not make this sort of change in earthquake-prone zones until you have checked with an engineer.

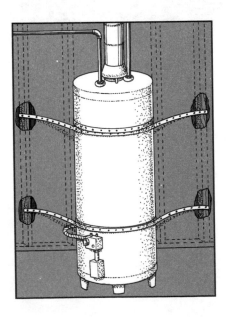

Use metal stripping to secure a water heater. Metal straps should be positioned at the top and about one third of the way up from the floor. Use 3-inch-long lag bolts to secure the strapping to wall studs. Gas water heaters should be connected to the supply line with a flexible pipe.

To prevent your water heater from toppling in an earthquake or storm, use metal strapping to secure the water heater to the wall. The metal straps should be positioned at the top and about one third of the way up the side (from the floor) of the water heater. Use 3-inch long lag bolts to secure the strapping to the wall studs. Also, for gas water heaters, install a flexible gas pipe to connect the heater to the gas supply pipe. The flexible pipe will let the water heater move without breaking the gas pipe.

Install wire-reinforced or other safety glass in your house. If the house already has ordinary window glass, have experts install a plastic film covering made by 3M Co. on the glass to eliminate the danger from shattered glass.

Install safety catches on cabinet doors and drawers. Check out the latches offered in your store's hardware section. Small plastic latches are available to "child proof" cabinets. These are inexpensive and are installed out of sight on the inside of the cabinet door or drawer.

Install several security night-lights to light an emergency exit path. These security lights have backup battery power in case the electrical power supply is interrupted.

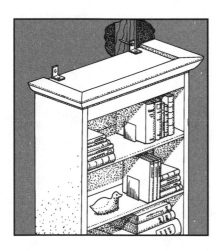

Install metal "L" brackets between furniture and wall studs at the top of tall bookcases.

113 EMERGENCY TOILET OR SEWER

Storm-caused damage to your house or to sanitary sewer facilities may leave you temporarily without toilet or sewer services. During earthquakes sewer and water pipes can be disrupted or disconnected. Plan in advance how to handle toilet needs until services are restored.

If toilet or other water drains are plugged, do not continue to run water or human waste into sinks or toilet bowls. You can use a camp toilet or Porta Potti in an emergency. If you have no camp toilet, you can make one by fitting a heavy-duty plastic trash bag into a plastic or metal pail or other container. If no other option is available, a plastic garbage pail can be used as a toilet. Use household bleach or disinfectant for odor control. Once used, dispose of the plastic bags by burying them, or by dumping the contents into the sewer when service is restored.

Another toilet option is to dig a military-type latrine. The latrine is simply a trench in the earth, dug two to three feet deep. To control odors and flies, spread a thin layer of dirt or lime over the wastes each time the latrine is used. Refill the trench with earth when the emergency period is over.

EMERGENCY COOKING AND HEATING

If you live in areas of extreme cold, where blizzards are common, you should have a backup heat source such as a fireplace or portable heater for emergency use. But, whatever the emergency, you will need an optional cooking fire and/or heat source.

Even though you may have a gas-operated barbecue grill, you may want to consider buying a charcoal grill for emergency use as a cookstove, when the gas supply may be interrupted. If you live in an area where natural disasters occur, at least consider storing a few bags of charcoal and a can of charcoal lighter. You don't necessarily need a charcoal grill. The charcoal can be spread on the ground, placed in a pit dug in the ground, or poured into a metal 5-gallon pail to provide heat for cooking or warmth. Observe normal precautions for open flames, however, and don't burn charcoal indoors without ventilation.

Other cooking and heating sources may be provided by camp stoves, (white) gas or propane lanterns, or even by candles placed in a coffee can. Be sure to keep a supply of matches in a waterproof container, and be aware of all the cooking/heating options on hand in case emergencies arise.

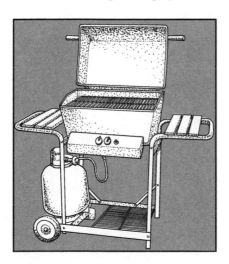

Camping stoves, barbecue grills, or a pile of charcoal can be used to cook food in an emergency.

115 EARTHQUAKES

When earthquakes occur, the primary danger is from being struck by falling materials as buildings or other structures collapse. If you are indoors when a quake occurs, move to a central hall or archway, where load-bearing walls or beams can help prevent roof or ceiling materials from falling on you. Or crawl under a sturdy table or desk to avoid falling plaster and joists.

Ruptured utility pipes (gas) or electrical lines are also hazards that can cause fire or explosion. If time permits, turn off utilities (see Shut Off House Utilities, p. 143) to avoid potential damage to the house. Because gas service should be restored only by a serviceman, experts advise that you turn off the gas *only* after the earthquake is over, and *only* if you smell gas or detect a leak in the line.

116 HAVE A PLAN FOR EMERGENCIES

To help the family act sensibly during any crisis, we should develop an emergency plan. The following plan is modified from one developed by the California Governor's Office of Emergency Services for use in earthquakes, but most of the same tips are useful in any natural emergency situation.

First, discuss the plan with the family, and be sure that all members understand the plan and the reasons for it. Hold practice drills as necessary to walk the family through all safety and evacuation procedures. Draw a floor plan of your home and locate the following:

- The safest places in the house.
- The most dangerous places.
- Exits and alternative exits—have at least two exit paths from upper floors and basements.
- Utility shutoff valves.
- Flashlights and batteries.
- First aid kit.
- Fire extinguishers.
- Food and water supplies.
- Transistor radio and batteries.

Also:

- Make needed special provisions for elderly or handicapped family members.
- Make evacuation plans for children's school or day care.
- Make provisions for pets in your home (pets will not be allowed in official shelters).
- Have a neighborhood plan to identify skills that are nearby, such as neighbors who are doctors, policemen, firemen, nurses, etc.
- Agree on a meeting place to head for if the family becomes separated. This could be a neighbor's house or a nearby facility such as a school or fire station.
- Also, if the family is separated, agree in advance upon a person outside the immediate area who will coordinate family contact. This could be a relative who lives in a distant city. Long distance phone service often is working long before local service is restored, so be sure everyone calls the chosen relative to check in.

 **BE PREPARED**

After a storm or earthquake is over, the danger has not yet passed. Daily services that we all take for granted—fire, police, and ambulance or other medical services—may be overextended, or the phones to summon them may be still. Stores may be inaccessible or sold out of ordinary necessities such as food, medicine, or health aids. Water service may be disrupted so even drinking water is not available. You should be prepared to survive in an emergency situation for a minimum of 3 days (72 hours) with no outside help.

Food. Most homes will contain enough food to last the family for three days, more is better. Experts suggest that, depending on the type of emergency, a family may need enough reserve foods to last up to two weeks. Make a point of stocking enough staples to see the family through. If electric service is out, frozen food will keep for up to three days if you keep the freezer door closed. Be careful to include in your pantry a supply of any specialty foods your family may need, such as infant formula or diabetic diet items.

Water. Although water service may be interrupted, you still should have some water available in the house. The water heater will hold 30 to 40 gallons of water. Turn the faucet at the bottom of the heater to draw out the water. There are also 5 to 7 gallons of water in the toilet flush tank or water closet. If water supplies dwindle, you can melt the ice cubes in the freezer or drain liquid from canned foods. Depending on the type of disaster you may face,

Keep an emergency food shelf stocked with canned food and water.

you may also want to have water purification tablets on hand. In flood areas, for example, water supplies are often contaminated. Buy purification tablets at stores that sell camping and outdoor supplies, or ask your pharmacist to obtain the tablets for you.

First Aid. Your home medicine cabinet should contain a supply of emergency medical supplies, including iodine or disinfectant, bandages, aspirin, and alcohol. It is also a good idea to have a first aid kit that contains a variety of medical needs and can be moved on short notice, along with a book on first aid. For those who take daily medication, don't neglect to include a supply of prescription drugs. Certainly the best preparation you can make for emergencies is to have all members of the family take a Red Cross class in first aid, and especially to learn CPR techniques.

Fire Extinguishers. Buy one or several fire extinguishers, be sure every responsible family member knows how to use them, and have the units serviced annually to be sure they are operational. Be sure the fire extinguishers are multipurpose, labeled ABC, to handle any kind of fire. Remember, there may be no professional fire service available if there is widespread community damage.

118 HOW TO PURIFY WATER

During emergencies such as earthquakes, floods, or hurricanes the normal water supply may be interrupted. As noted above (see Be Prepared, p. 160), there will be potable water (fit for human consumption) in the water heater, the toilet tank (if there is no disinfectant in the tank), or from melting ice cubes. If the fixtures are damaged, or if you use up all such stored water, you can purify water in several ways.

Before disaster strikes, turn on the valve or faucet at the bottom of the water heater tank and let the water run until it is free of rust or mineral sediment. Do this at least once per month so that water in the heater is clean enough to drink in case of emergency.

Buy water purification tablets from camping supply stores or from your local pharmacist. Keep the tablets handy in an emergency kit.

Polluted water can also be purified by boiling. Bring the water to a rolling boil and let it boil for 3–5 minutes. Then let the water cool. To aerate the water for better taste, pour the water rapidly back and forth between two containers several times.

If you have no water purification tablets, plain household bleach (5.25% sodium hypochlorite) can be added to water to make it safe for consumption. Store a gallon of plain bleach (no additives) and a measuring spoon or eyedropper. To purify one quart of water add four drops of bleach; for 1 gallon of water add 16 drops or ¼ teaspoon of bleach, and to purify 5 gallons of water add 1 teaspoon of bleach. Be sure to mix the water/bleach solution completely and let it stand for 30 minutes to be sure all bacteria is killed before drinking.

To purify water, boil it for several minutes or add 16 drops of sodium hypochlorite (bleach) to a gallon of water.

EMERGENCY FOOD

In an emergency, access to your normal food supplies may be cut off for days or even weeks. Experts suggest that an emergency food supply should be enough to last for two weeks. Canned food is the easiest food to store. Put together a two-week supply of the foods your family enjoys most. Canned soups, vegetables, and spaghetti can be heated and eaten from the cans. Include canned fruits and juices to balance the meals as best you can. Bottled or canned soft drinks and water should also be included. Be sure you have a manual can opener on hand.

Store salt, pepper, and sugar in plastic Tupperware containers. These sealable containers can also keep cookies, crackers, and snacks fresh for some time. Canned goods can usually be stored for up to one year, but you should rotate the food supply throughout the months, using the older foods first, to be sure the canned foods are wholesome and edible. In the event of power loss, fresh food that is refrigerated should be cooked or used immediately. If there is any doubt whether food is spoiled, don't risk food poisoning; discard it.

Food that is stored in the freezer normally will stay frozen for up to three days after electrical power is interrupted. Avoid opening the freezer door often when power is off, because food will thaw quickly if the space is opened to room temperatures. Finally, don't forget to include a supply of specialty foods, such as infant formula or canned baby foods, or diet items for any family member who has health problems. Also, don't overlook a supply of food for your pet.

WINTER WEATHER

If you live or travel in cold weather country, you should know and understand the words of winter warning. Weather forecasts of *freezing rain* or *freezing drizzle* mean a coating of ice should be expected on roads and walks, and driving or walking will be treacherous. *Flurries* mean only light snow; *snow* means a steady fall, and *heavy snow* means 6 or more inches of snow within the next 12 hours or 8 or more inches of snow in the next 24 hours can be expected. A *winter storm watch* means a winter storm is approaching or conditions exist for the development of a winter storm, and a *winter storm warning* means there is a high probability of approaching severe winter weather.

A prediction of an approaching *blizzard* means that one can expect heavy falling and/or blowing snow, with winds of 35 mph or greater velocity, which may reduce visibility down to one-quarter mile or less. Obviously, the ability to move about or to travel is greatly diminished during a blizzard because of drifting snow, extreme cold, or "wind chill factors", and the danger of becoming disoriented or lost due to limited visibility. The rule is to never leave shelter during blizzard conditions.

WIND CHILL CHART

Actual Thermometer Reading (°F.)

Estimated wind speed (in mph)	50	40	30	20	10	0	−10	−20	−30	−40	−50	−60
calm	50	40	30	20	10	0	−10	−20	−30	−40	−50	−60
5	48	37	27	16	6	−5	−15	−26	−36	−47	−57	−68
10	40	28	16	4	−9	−21	−33	−46	−58	−70	−83	−95
15	36	22	9	−5	−18	−36	−45	−58	−72	−85	−99	−112
20	32	18	4	−10	−25	−39	−53	−67	−82	−96	−110	−124
25	30	16	0	−15	−29	−44	−59	−74	−88	−104	−118	−133
30	28	13	−2	−18	−33	−48	−63	−79	−94	−109	−125	−140
35	27	11	−4	−20	−35	−49	−67	−82	−98	−113	−129	−145
40	26	10	−6	−21	−37	−53	−69	−85	−100	−116	−132	−148

(wind speeds greater than 40 mph have little additional effect)	LITTLE DANGER (for properly clothed person)	INCREASING DANGER	GREAT DANGER

(Danger from freezing of exposed flesh)

In conditions where severe cold temperatures combine with high winds, one must be alert for the wind chill factor (WCF). The *wind chill factor* refers to the affect of combined cold and wind on human skin. For example, if the temperature is zero and the wind is calm, the affect on the skin, or WCF, is simply zero. But if the temperature is zero and the wind speed is 20 mph, the skin will suffer frostbite or freezing as though the temperature were −39 degrees. This increased chance of frostbite to human skin is the wind chill factor. Frostbite dangers are much greater for the elderly or for those with poor circulation.

121 BLIZZARDS AT HOME

If you live in a rural area where electrical failures are common and utility service response time is long, consider having a gas-powered generator hooked directly into your house electrical service. A generator can provide enough electrical power to run water pumps for your well and power the electrical system on your furnace. In case of power outage it is also wise to have some type of portable heater that can be run without electricity. A pellet- or wood-burning stove or fireplace for alternative heat can become a lifesaver when electrical power fails.

Check battery-powered emergency equipment, including radios and lights, and keep a food stock of items that do not need refrigeration or cooking. Be cautious of fire. Stoves, furnaces, fireplaces, or heaters may become over-heated from trying to meet the emergency conditions and could pose a fire hazard. You don't want to add a house fire to the emergency of a blizzard.

If the heating system fails or you will be out in a car during extremely cold weather, remember that several layers of light clothing are warmer than a single layer of heavy clothing. Wear a hat, because most body heat escapes through the bare head. A good choice for headwear is a ski mask or knit cap. These are crushable and can be stuffed into any odd space. Ski masks also can cover the mouth to protect the lungs in extremely cold weather. If you are middle-aged and must go outside, wear a scarf, ski mask, or dust mask over your nose and mouth to prewarm the air you are breathing, be-cause breathing cold air seems to trigger heart attacks.

If you are over 50 years of age (some doctors say the limit should be 40 years of age), be cautious about shoveling snow or pushing a stuck car. Both chores are extremely hard work and can trigger a heart attack. Heart attacks are a major cause of death from winter storms.

EMERGENCY CAR KIT

If you live in a snow state or travel cross-country, it is wise to include a winter emergency kit in your car trunk. A kit for winter use is somewhat different from the car kits recommended for other emergency use. Items include:

- Flashlight, radio, and extra batteries.
- Two or more blankets and/or sleeping bags.
- Supply of matches and candles or solid fuel, packed in large coffee can(s).
- Extra winter clothing, including ski masks, mittens, boots, or overshoes. Remember that mittens (where fingers are in one pocket) are warmer than gloves (where fingers are covered but separated).
- Compass and maps.
- Pocket knife.
- First aid kit.
- Large box of facial tissues.
- Battery booster cables.
- Colorful signal cloth.
- Camping shovel.
- Compact alcohol stove.
- Supply of high-calorie, nonperishable food, can opener, spoons.

123 BLIZZARDS WHILE DRIVING

If you are driving in unfamiliar territory where blizzards can occur, keep the car radio tuned for weather information. Many snow states issue highway condition reports, or bulletins from the state highway patrol. When highway officials issue "no driving" or "emergency driving only" warnings, seek shelter in the nearest town or motel immediately. Be sure there is an emergency kit in the car, including extra clothing, blankets or sleeping bags, matches, and candles. Place the matches and candles in a 3-pound coffee can to keep them dry. If you become stranded, burn the candles inside the coffee can for light and heat. A small portable white gas or alcohol heater can save your life if you become stuck in drifted snow.

If the car becomes stuck, stay with the car. The car can be the best shelter you can find in a blizzard emergency. If you leave the car, you may become lost and unable to find your way back to the car.

In the prepared emergency kit you will have a handy signal cloth. The signal cloth should be either hot pink or blaze orange, the two most visible colors. If you have a bright signal cloth, raise the radio antenna to its highest point and tie the cloth to it. The cloth will stand out so searchers can spot it. At night, turn on the car's dome light to attract attention. With a window slightly open to ensure fresh air, and with the car's heater set on high, run the car engine for ten or fifteen minutes each hour to warm the car interior. To avoid carbon monoxide poisoning, be sure the exhaust system is in good shape and the exhaust tail pipe is not blocked by snow. To keep awake and to ensure good circulation, move about as much as possible. Clap your hands, change body position, keep feet elevated, and cuddle together to share body heat. Sleep in shifts, so someone in the car is awake to monitor conditions.

Melt snow for drinking water. A winter emergency kit should contain high-energy snack foods, because you burn more calories in cold weather. Shop camping stores to buy trail mix and other high-energy snack items to include in the food reserves. Be sure to keep change in the car so you can use remote pay phones.

124 LIGHTNING

At any given time 1,800 thunderstorms are occurring around the world. A typical lightning flash may generate 30 million volts and 25,000 amperes of electricity. The thunder you hear is an explosion of air at temperatures ranging from 30,000 to 50,000 degrees Fahrenheit. Because lightning usually kills only one or two people at a time, it does not seem a spectacular threat to most people, but it kills more people each year than hurricanes, tornadoes, and floods combined.

The safest refuges from lightning include buildings that are equipped with lightning protection, large steel-framed buildings, closed metal vehicles such as a car, and large frame buildings with nonconductive (wood) floors.

Indoor activities to avoid include talking on the telephone, any kitchen activities, bathing, doing laundry, watching TV, or standing in front of an open window or door. Stay away from metal pipes such as hot water heating pipes or plumbing drain stacks. Lightning can travel through these pipes and side-flash to a person's chest area. These direct side-flash hits are often fatal.

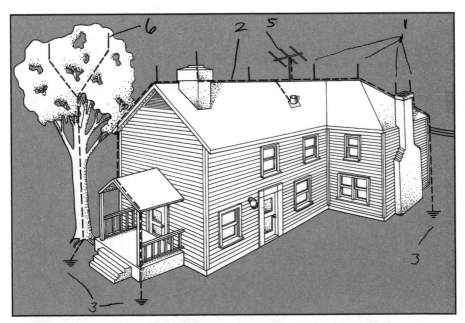

Professionals can install lightning protection for your house. In the illustration, (1) indicates air terminals; (2) indicates cable; (3) indicates ground rod; (4) and (5) are secondary service arresters that should protect antennas, chimneys, etc; (6) tree protection.

Outdoor locations to avoid during lightning storms include unprotected (by lighting equipment) shelters in parks or on golf courses, open fields, lone trees, taller trees in woods, and wire fences. Don't swim. Dismount from your horse, bicycle, golf cart, or lawn tractor.

If you are caught in an open area, kneel down and bend low to the ground. Touch the ground only with the knees and feet. Keep arms folded at your side, and do not touch the hands to the knees.

If someone has been struck by lightning, check to see if there is a pulse. There should be a detectable pulse in the neck and tonsil area, below the ear. If a pulse is found, apply mouth-to-mouth resuscitation. If no pulse is found, use heart compression plus mouth-to-mouth resuscitation (CPR techniques) to revive the victim. Summon medical help as quickly as possible.

125 VOLTAGE SURGE SUPPRESSORS

Indoors, surges or spikes in electrical power can damage electronic gear, including TVs, VCRs, computers, microwave ovens, and home security systems. Be sure this valuable equipment is protected from power surges.

When lightning strikes occur near an electric power line, an induced surge of voltage may occur on the line. This surge is a sudden blip or increase in the current on the line. Electric power companies install devices called lightning arresters on their power transmission lines to protect transformers and other equipment from damage. The arresters are designed to trap or reduce the voltage surge on the power lines and to protect the power company's equipment. In addition to lightning strikes, transient power surges in the home can result from use of motorized appliances or when electric service is restored after a power outage.

Some appliances, such as color TVs, may have built-in surge suppressors. Devices called lightning surge arresters can be installed on the home's electrical service panel to protect house wiring and appliances from electrical spikes or surges. These devices are installed near the electric meter and will direct excess power to ground before it can harm the wiring system or appliances. One power company (Northern States Power in Minneapolis, Minnesota) quotes a price between $180 and $195 to install their arrester, Surge Guard, in a home system.

Protect sensitive electronic equipment such as VCRs, stereos, or personal computers with surge suppressors that can be plugged into any conventional wall outlet and will trap voltage spikes before they can damage the equipment. The individual surge suppressors are available at most electronics or computer stores, or ask your power company to install them.

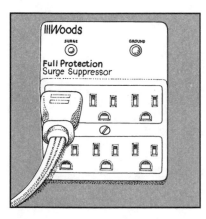

Voltage surge suppressors plug into existing outlets and protect expensive electronic equipment from spikes in electrical current.

171

CHAPTER NINE

125

TOOLS

TIPS

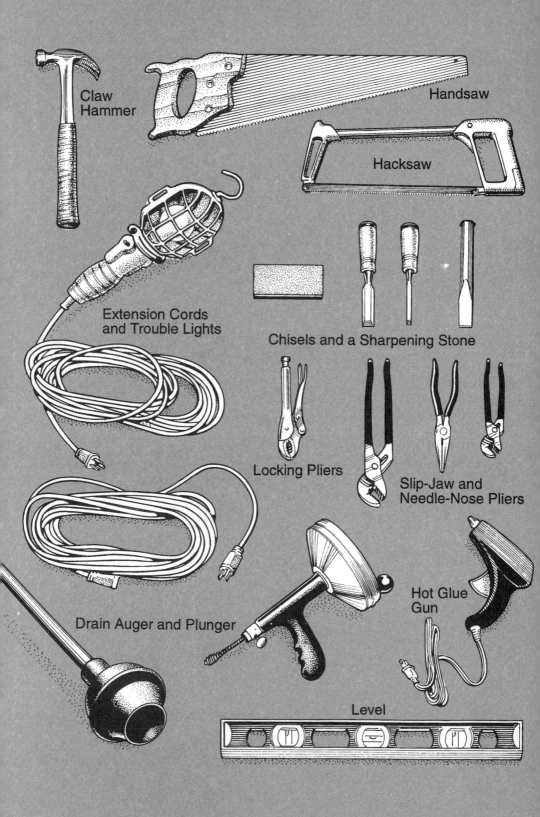

Claw Hammer

Handsaw

Hacksaw

Extension Cords and Trouble Lights

Chisels and a Sharpening Stone

Locking Pliers

Slip-Jaw and Needle-Nose Pliers

Hot Glue Gun

Drain Auger and Plunger

Level

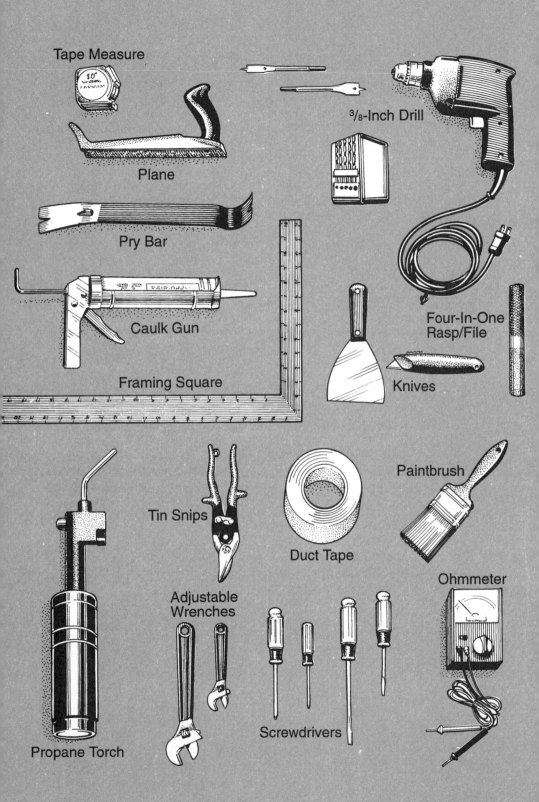

Tape Measure

Plane

³/₈-Inch Drill

Pry Bar

Caulk Gun

Framing Square

Four-In-One Rasp/File

Knives

Tin Snips

Duct Tape

Paintbrush

Ohmmeter

Adjustable Wrenches

Propane Torch

Screwdrivers

To accomplish basic repairs—along with more urgent ones—every homeowner should have on hand a set of essential tools. With reasonable care most quality tools will last a lifetime. To ensure that this happens, follow a few simple guidelines.

Always use a tool for the job it was designed for, and never use a tool that you want to keep in good shape for a project that may bend, dull, or otherwise impair its ability to work the way it should. When using tools around water, always dry them after the job is completed or at the end of the day. Apply a light coating of oil to metal tool parts with a rag. Remove any rust by rubbing the affected area with a piece of steel wool dipped in a solvent such as kerosene. Remove sawdust from motor vents on power tools.

You may not need or want all the tools we've compiled here, but you'll probably find the need for most at one time or another. You might buy the basics now and add the specialty tools later when you need them. Here's a selection, along with a few words on each tool's features and most likely uses.

CLAW HAMMER

A good finishing hammer will last a lifetime and help you through a wide variety of improvement and repair projects. A hammer with a steel or fiberglass handle will be the most durable, especially when pulling nails. One with a curved claw and a 1-pound head is best. This combination will work well on rough carpentry as well as finish work. A quality hammer can mean the difference between driving nails and bending them.

HANDSAW

Next on your list will be a good crosscut saw. Handsaws cost a good deal less than powered saws and work just as well in limited-used situations. You'll also be able to reach into spaces too cramped for a circular saw. A 10-point crosscut saw, having ten teeth points per inch, will serve you well around the house and yard. This saw will cut clean enough for most finish work and quickly enough for most rough work. If you'll be doing mostly rough carpentry, a 6- or 8-point saw will speed your work greatly.

HACKSAW

There are many occasions when a hacksaw comes in handy, from cutting plumbing pipes to trimming downspouts and slicing through ceramic tile. The most important thing to look for is rigidity. A saw that flexes when used will bend or break the blade, or will simply refuse to cut straight. Most are adjustable and will accept 10- or 12-inch blades. Look for a brand that provides for two different blade installations, either straight or at a 45° angle.

TAPE MEASURE

The best advice for selecting a tape measure is to avoid the short and narrow. For general household use, choose one that is at least ¾ inch wide and 15 feet long, and clips to a belt or pocket. And remember, a broken tape does not always mean a ruined tape measure. Replacement tapes are available for most brands.

PLANE

For trimming marginal thicknesses of lumber, consider buying a plane. As planes require exact adjustment and dull easily when used by untrained hands, a Surform-type tool is a good household alternative. This type of plane has a replaceable, slotted blade that gouges out narrow ribbons of wood, plastic, vinyl, and even aluminum, all without clogging. Unlike other planes, it will not yield the clean, hard-edged surface of a block plane, but it's a snap to use.

⅜-INCH DRILL

Another tool that will quickly earn its keep is a ⅜-inch drill. While cordless drills are ideal for the quick fix, a cord-type drill is more versatile. And because you won't be paying for a charger, you'll get more power per dollar invested. Look for one with a variable-speed, reversible motor capable of at least 2,000 rpm. The one we chose has 2.8 amps of power and offers an industry-standard 1-year warranty.

You'll also want a selection of drill bits and possibly a few specialty attachments. We chose a 13-piece, high-speed bit set with sizes graduating from ¹⁄₁₆ to ¼ inch. Buying bits in a case makes selection easier and also reveals at a glance which sizes you'll need to replace. Also, ½- and ¾-inch spade bits are useful for boring larger holes in wood, and are easily resharpened. A ⅜-inch drill also accepts a variety of bits and attachments such as a magnetized nut driver that drives self-tapping sheet-metal screws.

EXTENSION CORDS AND TROUBLE LIGHTS

To keep your projects well powered and better lighted, you'll need a grounded extension cord and a trouble light. A drop cord in the 30- to 50-foot category will serve most needs, but don't skimp on its wire size. A lightweight cord will allow too much voltage drop, which will in turn shorten the life of the tool or appliance it serves. Generally speaking, the longer the cord the heavier it will need to be.

As for trouble lights, look for models with 16-gauge wire. If the light you fancy does not have a receptacle, an ungrounded cord will do.

CHISELS AND A SHARPENING STONE

Every household should have a chisel or two for roughing out of wood or drywall that can't be reached with a larger, more precise tool. And, as many of us can blunt the edges of chisels just by picking them up, you'll also want a double-sided (fine/course) sharpening stone. When used with honing oil, a sharpening stone will resharpen the edges of all but the most abused chisels and knives.

You'll need to decide which sizes best suit your purposes, but two will often do. We chose ¼- and ¾-inch chisels and a 5 × 2-inch combination stone.

And finally, you may want a cold chisel in your toolbox for those materials not made of wood. A cold chisel can be used to chip concrete or split light-gauge metal. It's especially handy for cutting bricks, blocks, and paving stones.

FRAMING SQUARE

A framing square in the hands of a professional can work wonders, but even a beginner will find this a useful tool, if only as straightedge and angle finder. It can be used to check the squareness of a room before laying floor coverings or to ensure a square cut in plywood or dimensional lumber. They are available in steel and aluminum.

CAULK GUN

With everything from caulk and glue to grout and roofing tar packaged in tubes these days, a good caulk gun is a must. Expect to find two or three levels of quality in caulk guns. Go right past the bargain basket to those in the mid-priced range that will accommodate all ¹⁄₁₀-gallon tubes and are sturdy enough for years of casual use.

PRY BAR

A pry bar is another useful tool, with more real-life uses than its manufacturers probably intended. A pry bar is designed to pry things apart, primarily pieces of wood. It is equipped with beveled nail claws at each end and has a curved shank ending in a sharp right angle. When a block of wood is placed under one end, it makes a great lever and fulcrum.

KNIVES

Everyone is familiar with the uses of a putty knife, but when you head out to buy one, consider upsizing to a 4-inch drywall knife for greater versatility. A flexible drywall knife can be used to apply spackling, scrape paint, strip furniture, or press wallpaper into corners. Make sure that the model you choose has a chrome-plated blade to resist corrosive drywall compounds.

You'll also want a sturdy utility knife for cutting open cartons, trimming wallpaper and floor coverings, and for a dozen other chores. We suggest a knife with a retractable blade for easier and safer storage.

FOUR-IN-ONE RASP/FILE

You might also consider purchasing a combination wood rasp and file for your tool kit. With both a course and fine rasp, as well as a course and fine file on each tool, you'll be able to shape wood and sharpen garden tools whenever the need arises.

LOCKING PLIERS

Locking pliers first became popular in shipyards during World War II. Before long they found their way into just about every mechanic's toolbox and have lately turned up in a good many kitchen drawers as well. This tool is so popular because it can do so much. It's a plier, a makeshift wrench, a wire cutter, *and* a sturdy clamp.

SLIP-JAW AND NEEDLE-NOSE PLIERS

Slip-jaw pliers make a good choice because the jaws are able to expand to meet the job requirements. Their offset jaw configuration also provides a little more leverage than standard pliers. We decided on two sizes, a 6½- and a 10-inch model. The smaller pliers are good for small household projects, while the larger version will easily handle the chrome or plastic trap nuts on plumbing fixtures. With new home construction including almost all plastic pipes and fittings, this size makes a good substitute for a standard pipe wrench. Eight-inch needle-nose pliers have a long reach for getting into cramped spaces, which is where needle-nose pliers work best. Most have a wire cutter built into the jaws.

DRAIN AUGER AND PLUNGER

There's a perverse physical law that has drains clogging only when plumbers and drain services are hard to reach, and if you are lucky enough to find one that will answer your call for help quickly, the job will likely be frightfully expensive. Drain clogs like holidays best.

For those times and others, plan ahead and invest in an inexpensive drain auger. Avoid the simple, bare-cable type augers; they won't give enough cranking power in problem situations.

A plunger is the other half of the clogged drain solution. Most clogs can be broken free with a good plunger, almost to the complete exclusion of caustic chemicals. Look for one that has a large cup with a folding funnel. With the funnel folded in, this plunger will work well on sinks and tubs. Folded out, it's perfect for toilet clogs. Avoid purchasing smaller plungers. While they're easy to store, you'll get little clog-busting force out of them.

In addition to these tools, you may also want to include a pipe wrench to round out your plumbing tool needs and forestall other difficulties later.

HOT GLUE GUN

Hot glue guns used to be hobby tools, but more and more of us are finding them useful around the house. They work especially well in repairing small fittings on toys and other household items, especially plastics. Best of all, hot glue sets as soon as it cools, which can speed things up substantially. You'll find inexpensive versions that are fed simply by pushing the glue stick through the gun. Others feature a trigger-feed mechanism that offers better control when applying the glue.

LEVEL

A good 2-foot level is another tool you'll find yourself using over and over again. It can level picture frames, start wallpaper, measure short items, level appliances, and provide a straightedge for a knife or pencil. You'll find them made of steel, aluminum, plastic, and wood. The metal versions offer the most versatility and strength for the money.

PROPANE TORCH

When making emergency plumbing repairs, a propane torch will put the most distance between you and a professional plumber. As a skill, soldering is largely overrated. But you will need a torch. You'll find two varieties in home centers. One will require that you light it with a striker or match. The other is self-starting. Just turn it on and pull the

trigger for a clean blue flame. Purchase a small tin of flux and a roll of lead-free solder along with the torch. (The EPA has prohibited the use of high-lead solders in plumbing since 1986.) Many torches come with soldering instructions. Read the instructions and practice with a few fittings and some copper pipe. If you buy a self-cleaning flux, you won't even need to sand the pipe and fittings.

TIN SNIPS

Tin snips may seem at the outer edge of tool selection, but when you need them there's no substitute. Try cutting an extra heat register in an unfinished basement without them. If the need arises, choose a pair designed to cut along a straight line. They can be made to cut wide, sweeping curves as well.

While you're at it, buy a 2-inch wide, 60-yard long roll of quality duct tape. You may never need it for duct-work, but you'll find a use for it just about everywhere else.

PAINTBRUSH

When it comes to paintbrushes, don't skimp. Cheap throwaways have a way of finding their own revenge. The material your brush is made from should be determined by your choice of paint. A brush with polyester or nylon bristles is suitable for latex or oil paint.

If you're going to buy one brush, make it polyester. Brushes made from hog bristle are best used with oil paints and get limp when used with latex paint. Good quality bristle brushes are expensive. Don't buy inexpensive bristle brushes; they lose their bristles. For a quick touch-up, use a small, inexpensive foam brush. Don't load it with too much paint; these brushes have a habit of dripping.

Consider brush shape when you're

buying supplies. Brushes are available with tapered or straight bristles. The straight cuts work best on large areas, while the tapered versions work better as trim brushes. You may need both, but a straight bristle brush is a good start.

ADJUSTABLE WRENCHES

A 6-inch wrench will work well in tightening furniture bolts, toilet bolts, appliance leveling legs, and the like. A 10-inch spanner will handle many plumbing repairs and do double duty in automotive work. Adjustable wrenches are available at several price levels. Avoid the low-end imports like the plague; midpriced versions should serve you quite well for many years.

SCREWDRIVERS

Screwdrivers are typically the most abused tools going. As such, steer clear of bargain-priced screwdrivers. Look for handles that are large enough to be comfortable and shanks that are long enough to let you see your work. The better brands will have hardened steel tips and may be magnetized. We recommend two Phillips-head and two slotted-head screwdrivers in small and medium sizes.

OHMMETER

An ohmmeter is a good choice if you plan to handle your own electrical problems. With it, you'll be able to test for voltage, continuity, and ohm levels. It can be used for checking out your home's electrical system, both wiring and devices, as well as the appliances within your home. An ohmmeter will tell you if a switch is defective (by checking continuity), or if the problem lies elsewhere.

In addition to an ohmmeter, you'll also want to have on hand several other tools when undertaking electrical work.

A voltage tester consists of two probes joined by a tiny neon light. It is commonly used to determine whether power is present in a set of wires or a receptacle. Also purchase a continuity tester, which will help you in testing if a switch or circuit is in operating condition. A continuity tester differs from a voltage tester in that it has a power source—a small battery. When the alligator clip at one end of the tester is touched to the probe at the other end, a circuit is completed and the light within the tester lights up in the handle. In like fashion, any device placed between the clip and probe will complete the circuit if it is in operating order.

GLOSSARY

airlock A blockage in a pipe caused by a trapped bubble of air.

alkyd paint An oil-based paint made of alkyd and other synthetic resins, slower drying but more durable than latex paint.

appliance A machine or device powered by electricity. Or a functional piece of equipment connected to the plumbing—a basin, sink, bath, etc.

asbestos A component in many building materials. May be hazardous to health if airborne particles are inhaled.

batten A narrow strip of wood.

bleeder valve A valve on one side of a radiator that can be loosened to let trapped air escape from the heating system.

circuit A complete path through which an electrical current can flow.

conductor A component, usually a length of wire, along which an electrical current will pass.

cordless tool Battery powered, rechargeable power tools that are safe to use when working around water and other damp locations.

countersink To cut a tapered recess which allows the head of a screw to lie flush with a surface. Also the tapered recess itself.

creosote A tarlike substance produced when wood burns in a fireplace that itself can become a fire hazard if allowed to build up in a chimney.

damper A paddlelike device inside a duct that regulates airflow to different parts of a house in a forced-air system.

drain valve A spigot at the base of a water heater that releases water when opened.

drywall Prefabricated panels consisting of a gypsum core surrounded by a paper cover used for walls and ceilings in home interiors.

efflorescence A white powdery deposit caused by soluble salts migrating to the surface of masonry.

Elder Alert A kit designed for the safety of seniors whereby critical medical information is stored in a tube placed in a refrigerator.

enhanced 911 The universal emergency number with the added feature of providing the location, telephone number, and the name of the person listed under that number when 911 is dialed.

film badge sensor A type of carbon monoxide detector that is placed in the immediate area around a furnace.

flashing A weatherproof junction between a roof and a wall or chimney, or between one roof and another.

frost line The depth to which the soil freezes in a given locale.

fuse box Where the main electrical service cable is connected to the house circuitry. Also the service panel.

galvanized Covered with a protective coating of zinc that prevents rust.

GFCI (ground fault circuit interrupter) A very sensitive device that quickly shuts down electrical current to prevent accidental shock.

greenfield cable The flexible steel tubing that grounds the electrical system in an older wiring scheme.

grommet A ring of rubber or plastic lining a hole to protect electrical cable from chafing.

grout A ready-mixed paste used when tiling to fill in the gaps between the tiles.

hardwood Timber cut from deciduous trees.

insulation Materials used to reduce the transmission of heat or sound. Also the nonconductive material surrounding electrical wires or connections to prevent the passage of electricity.

joist A horizontal wooden or metal beam used to support a structure like a floor or ceiling.

latex paint The most common water-based paint. Faster drying and easier to work with than oil-based (alkyd) paints but not as durable.

metal paint Either an alkyd or latex paint containing zinc or other rust inhibitors.

miter A joint formed between two pieces of wood by cutting bevels of equal angles at the ends of each piece. Also to cut such a joint.

motion detector A device that incorporates an infrared beam of light that, when interrupted by an obstruction or person, activates lighting, stops an automatic garage door, or sets off an alarm.

nail pop The exposure of a nail head in the surface in which it is embedded, leaving a gap between the two. Often a problem with drywall installation and wooden decks.

oxidize To form a layer of metal oxide; to rust.

pigtail wire A small length of wire connected to a longer length with a plastic connector. Often used in electrical work to ground an outlet, switch, or fixture.

pressure-treated wood Lumber that is resistant to decay and insect damage, against which it is normally guaranteed.

primer The first coat of a paint system to protect the work piece and reduce absorption of subsequent coats.

PRV (pressure relief valve) A drainage pipe designed to discharge water that has risen above its intended level in a water heater.

radon A naturally occurring radioactive gas that may be harmful if large concentrations are found in a home.

radon detector A device that reveals if radon is present in a home.

Romex cable   Standard cable for to-day's wiring. Romex cable contains three wires wrapped in insulation.

service panel   The point where the main electrical service cable is connected to the house circuits. Circuit breakers protect individual circuits in the system. Sometimes called a beaker box.

sheathing   The outer layer of insulation surrounding an electrical cable. Also the outer covering of a stud-framed wall that is applied beneath the wall siding.

short circuit   The accidental rerouting of electricity to ground, which increases the flow of current and either blows a fuse or trips a circuit breaker.

soffit   The underside of a part of a building, such as the eaves, archway, etc.

splashblock   A troughlike device placed under ground pipes or downspouts that directs water away from the house.

stucco   A thin layer of cement-based mortar applied to the exterior walls to provide a protective finish. Sometimes fine stone aggregate is embedded in the mortar. Also, to apply the mortar.

stud   The vertical member of a stud-framed wall.

Teflon tape   Material that is wrapped around the threads of pipe fittings to prevent water and gas leaks.

template   A cutout pattern to help shape something accurately.

thinner   A solvent used to dilute paint or varnish.

torque   A rotational force.

trap   A bent section of pipe containing standing water to prevent the passage of gases; sometimes called a P-trap.

TSP (trisodium phosphate)   A powerful detergent used primarily for cleaning asphalt and stone surfaces.

voltage surge suppressor   A device that protects electronic equipment such as televisions and computers from sudden voltage spikes.

water hammer   A vibration in plumbing pipework caused by fluctuating water pressure.

wax ring   The circular gasket at the base of a toilet stool that prevents leakage of waste and water.

weather radio   A radio tuned to frequencies where weather forecasts by the National Oceanic and Atmospheric Administration (NOAA) can be heard 24 hours a day.

weather stripping   A special molding fitted at the bottom of an exterior door to prevent moisture and the flow of air underneath.

wire nut   A common brand of plastic connector used to join electrical wire.

SOURCES

You may want to contact one of the professional associations or organizations for information. They may also be helpful in answering questions you might have about standards and business practices.

American Institute of Architects
1735 New York Ave., N.W.
Washington, D.C. 20006
(202) 626-7300

American Lighting Association
435 N. Michigan Ave., Suite 1717
Chicago, Ill. 60611
(312) 644-0828

American Plywood Association
P.O. Box 11700
Tacoma, Wa. 98411
(206) 565-6600

American Society of Interior Designers
608 Massachusetts Ave., N.E.
Washington, D.C. 20002
(202) 546-3480

Asbestos Information Association
1745 Jefferson Davis Hwy., Suite 509
Arlington, Va. 22202
(703) 979-1150

Association of Home Appliance
Manufacturers
20 N. Wacker Dr.
Chicago, Ill. 60606
(312) 984-5800

Floor Covering Installation
Contractors Association
P.O. Box 948
Dalton, Ga. 30722
(404) 226-5488

Independent Electrical Contractors
317 S. Patrick St.
Alexandria, Va. 22314
(703) 549-7351

International Association of Lighting
Designers
30 W. 22nd St., 4th Floor
New York, N.Y. 10010
(212) 206-1281

National Association of Home Builders
15th and M Sts., N.W.
Washington, D.C. 20005
(202) 822-0200

National Association of Plumbing,
Heating & Cooling Contractors
P.O. Box 6808
Falls Church, Va. 22040
(703) 237-8100

National Association of the
Remodeling Industry
4301 N. Fairfax Dr., Suite 310
Arlington, Va. 22203
(703) 276-7600

National Kitchen and Bath Association
687 Willow Grove St.
Hackettstown, N.J. 07840
(908) 852-0033

INDEX